MILTON'S *Paradise Lost*

MILTON'S
Paradise Lost

A COMMENTARY ON THE ARGUMENT

By John S. Diekhoff

You, therefore, who wish to remain
free, either instantly be wise, or
as soon as possible, cease to be
fools. — THE SECOND DEFENCE

1963
Humanities Press
New York

Printed in U.S.A. by
NOBLE OFFSET PRINTERS, INC.
NEW YORK 3, N. Y.

To

ANDREW BONGIORNO

and

GEORGE BRUNER PARKS

Table of Contents

CHAPTER I

Milton's Theory of Poetry

ACCORDING TO the theory of poetry that Milton accepted, the poet and the orator share the desire to move men to virtuous action. Persuasion, the chief end of oratory, is also part of the function of poetry.

The defenses of poetry that were written in England in the sixteenth century were written in answer to Puritan charges of immorality. These defenses devoted themselves generally to the affirmation of the moral value of poetry, finding arguments ready to hand not only in classical critics and rhetoricians, but also in the writings of the Italian Renaissance critics—Minturno and Scaliger most notably. For Milton, poetry, unlike the Smectymnuans, unlike the people of England, unlike himself, needed no apology and no defense. But his conception of poetry is very like that of its defenders. He accepted as a partial statement of the end of poetry the Renaissance version of the Horatian statement that the aim of the poet is either to profit or to delight, or to be at once pleasant and profitable. The critics of the Renaissance, or many of them, chose to minimize half of this statement—that poetry must please—in order to stress the other half—that poetry must be morally profitable. They chose also to ignore the reason Horace gives for his judgment a few lines later, that old men reject works which are not instructive, and young men those which are not lively, whereas the poet who is at once delightful and instructive pleases all, makes a fortune for the booksellers, and establishes his own fame.[1]

[1] *Ad Pisonem,* 333–334, 342–346.

The concern of the English defenders of poetry was not, like that of Horace, to sell books and make the poet more or less immortal, but rather to justify buying and reading books. Their opponents were the old men of whom Horace speaks. But these English old men not only rejected particular poems that were void of instruction; they rejected poetry generally as void of instruction or because it sometimes instructs in evil. The defenders' problem was to show on the contrary that poetry has a reforming power and that that power is enhanced by the accompanying power to please. Sidney, combining into a single sentence Aristotle's definition of poetry as an imitation, Plutarch's metaphor of the "speaking picture," and the Horatian statement of the dual purpose not of poetry but of poets, describes "poesie" as

an arte of imitation, for so Aristotle termeth it in his word Mimesis, that is to say, a representing, counterfeiting, or figuring forth: to speak metaphorically, a speaking picture: with this end, to teach and delight.

To Sidney's mind, the purpose of the poet in delighting his reader is to make his teaching more effective, for "right poets"

indeede doo meerely make to imitate, and imitate both to delight and teach, and delight to move men to take that goodness in hand, which without delight they would flye as from a stranger. . . .

Again, of the poet:

For he dooth not only show the way, but giveth so sweete a prospect into the way, as will intice any man to enter into it.

For Milton, too, following the same Classical and Italian critics and having read Sidney also, the chief function of poetry is to instruct. We should know this, of course, from his choice of themes for his four narrative poems if from no other evidence. The poems speak for themselves in the matter, but there is also a fully developed theory of poetry behind Milton's practice.

The attack on literature of the Elizabethan Puritans was

aimed, of course, at literature at its worst—at its moral worst. Sidney and the other critics who came to its defense ignored the worst and defended poetry at its best. Milton differs from them in not ignoring the existence of bad, of vicious poetry, and does not choose to defend poetry generally. He describes it at its best, however, and his description is very like the traditional "defense." The dual function of poetry is to teach and to delight. The danger inherent in the writings of "libidinous and ignorant Poetasters" lies in their ability to teach ill. From them, who "lap up vitious principles in sweet pils to be swallow'd down, and make the tast of vertuous documents harsh and sowr," the "youth and gentry" are liable to suck in daily corruption and bane.[2] The true poet's business, on the contrary, is to teach the good. His first function is to instruct or edify. This implication is clear in the statement that the purpose of *Paradise Lost* is to "assert Eternal Providence,/ And justifie the wayes of God to men." It is clear in the *Apology for Smectymnuus,* where Milton expresses his preference of Dante and Petrarch to the "smooth Elegiack Poets" because Dante and Petrarch "never write but honour of them to whom they devote their verse, displaying sublime and pure thoughts, without transgression,"[3] and in the statement in *Areopagitica* that Spenser is a "better teacher than Scotus or Aquinas." Finally it is very clear indeed in the extended discussion of Milton's poetic aspirations in the *Reason of Church Government,* notably in the discussion of the possible forms into which Milton's projected great work may be cast. In this passage Milton bases his consideration of writing tragic rather than epic verse upon the question "whether those Drama-

[2] "The Reason of Church Government," *The Works of John Milton,* ed. Frank A. Patterson and others (New York, 18 vols., Columbia University Press, 1931–1938), III, Pt. I, 239. Hereafter reference will be made to this as Columbia *Milton.* All quotations from Milton are from this edition.

[3] Columbia *Milton,* III, Pt. I, 302–303.

tick constitutions, wherein *Sophocles* and *Euripides* raigne shall be found more doctrinal and exemplary to a Nation." [4]

But Milton is not content merely to affirm that it is the business of poetry to teach; he is concerned also with the question of what it teaches and how. What it teaches is the whole of morality:

These abilities [of the poet], wheresoever they be found, are the inspired guift of God rarely bestow'd, but yet to some (though most abuse) in every Nation: and are of power beside the office of a pulpit, to inbreed and cherish in a great people the seeds of vertu, and publick civility, to allay the perturbations of the mind, and set the affections in right tune, to celebrate in glorious and lofty Hymns the throne and equipage of Gods Almightinesse, and what he works, and what he suffers to be wrought with high providence in his Church, to sing the victorious agonies of Martyrs and Saints, the deeds and triumphs of just and pious Nations doing valiantly through faith against the enemies of Christ, to deplore the general relapses of Kingdoms and States from justice and Gods true worship. Lastly, whatsoever in religion is holy and sublime, in vertu amiable, or grave, whatsoever hath passion or admiration in all the changes of that which is call'd fortune from without, or the wily suttleties and refluxes of mans thoughts from within, all these things with a solid and treatable smoothnesse to paint out and describe. Teaching over the whole book of sanctity and vertu . . .[5]

For Milton, as for other Renaissance critics before him—Minturno, Scaliger, Rainolds, Sidney, and Ben Jonson, for instance—poetry must delight in order that its teaching be effective. The discussion in the *Reason of Church Government* proceeds:

Teaching over the whole book of sanctity and vertu through all the instances of example with such delight to those especially of soft and delicious temper who will not so much as look upon Truth herselfe, unlesse they see her elegantly drest, that whereas the paths of honesty and good life appear now rugged and difficult, though they be indeed easy and pleasant, they would then appear to all men both easy and pleasant though they were rugged and difficult indeed.[6]

The end of poetry, then, is not only knowledge and pleasure

[4] *Ibid.,* p. 237.   [5] *Ibid.,* pp. 238–239.   [6] *Ibid.*

but action as well. It not only shows the way, "but giveth so sweete a prospect into the way, as will intice any man to enter into it." The aim of poetry is not as we have thus far described it, twofold, but threefold. The critics of the Renaissance, Sidney and Milton with them, have gone beyond Horace's statement that poets aim either to teach or to please, or to do both, and have given to poets the aims set down for orators by Cicero: to teach, to please, and to move. They are to persuade as well as to instruct.

The science of persuasion is not poetics but rhetoric: and it is clear that the theory of poetry we have outlined as Milton's is a fusion of rhetorical and poetic principles. Naturally enough. The critic who thinks that the function of poetry includes the function of oratory will not begrudge the poet the orator's methods. The poet schooled in rhetoric will use them.

For Aristotle, and hence for the classical scholars of the Renaissance, and for Milton, rhetoric is a counterpart of dialectic. What in dialectic is inductive reasoning finds its rhetorical counterpart in the example, the single instance illustrative of a principle, from which a principle may be induced. What in dialectic is deductive reasoning, syllogistic in form, in rhetoric becomes the enthymeme. But in addition to these two forms of proof, rhetoric—drawing upon all the means available—makes use of two means of persuasion that are not directed toward the intellect and hence are not proof in the strict sense of the word. Thus Aristotle:

Of the modes of persuasion furnished by the spoken word there are three kinds. The first kind depends on the personal character of the speaker; the second on putting the audience into a certain frame of mind; the third on the proof, or apparent proof, provided by the words of the speech itself.[7]

[7] Rhetorica, i. 2, in *The Works of Aristotle,* tr. W. Rhys Roberts, ed. W. D. Ross (Oxford, 1924), Vol. XI.

The speaker employs one of these nonlogical means, then, when he asserts his own authority, demonstrates his qualification to speak on the subject in hand, shows himself to be well-disposed toward his audience, or otherwise attempts to secure the sympathetic attention of that audience. He employs the other when he undertakes to enlist the emotions of his audience, to arouse admiration or affection for the protagonist, hate for the antagonist.

Milton uses all of these means of persuasion in *Paradise Lost,* and it is clear that he recognized the kinship between poem and oration. It would not be impossible to classify under the headings of the three types of oration recognized by classical rhetoric— the deliberative, the epideictic, and the forensic—the various tasks described in the paragraph we have quoted at length from the *Reason of Church Government* as within the scope of poetry. It is enough to observe, however, that since the ultimate value of poetry as a body, and therefore of poems in particular, is in terms of the result in action, the poet may be taken to be not poet (maker or imitator) alone, but a sort of deliberative orator as well. That in hymning "the throne and equipage of Gods Almightinesse" or in singing the "victorious agonies of Martyrs and Saints," poetry seems nearer akin to epideictic oratory; that in deploring "the general relapses of Kingdoms and States from justice and Gods true worship," or in justifying to men God's ways, it seems nearer to forensic oratory, does not really disturb this conclusion, for the end assigned to these poems, as to all others, is also to make the paths of honesty and the good life appear easy and pleasant in order to entice men into them.

The method of instruction particularly adapted to the uses of poetry is the method of example. Precept is used in lesser proportion than in philosophy and oratory. The choice of drama or epic, we have seen, was in terms not only of which form was the more doctrinal, but also which the more "exemplary." In the *Apology* for *Smectymnuus* the true poet is described in terms of the true poem, which is a "composition, and patterne of the best and honourablest things." [8] Spenser is praised in *Areopagitica* for his use of the example of Guyon, and in the passage we have quoted from the *Reason of Church Government* the book of sanctity and virtue is described as taught "through all the instances of example."

That this is not only Milton's view, but is in the best tradition of Renaissance criticism as well, Donald Clark shows conclusively in his study of *Rhetoric and Poetry in the Renaissance*. Clark cites utterances of half a dozen Italian Renaissance critics and concludes his discussion of "Rhetorical Elements in Italian Renaissance Conceptions of the Purpose of Poetry" by citing the view of Minturno and Scaliger that both a poem and a speech (the summary is Clark's):

endeavored to teach, to please, and to move. Both looked toward persuasion as an object. The speech used the enthymeme and the example as proofs, while the poem used the example to a greater, and the enthymeme to a lesser degree.

Clark concludes his chapter as follows:

Thus by the end of the sixteenth century, the Italian critics had formulated a logical and self-consistent theory of the purpose of poetry. Inheritors of the allegorical theory of the middle ages, which they in part discarded, and discoverers of classical rhetoric which they carried over bodily into their theories of poetry, they passed on to France, Germany, and England their rhetorical theories. The purpose of poetry, as well as of rhetoric, was to them persuasion—to teach, to please, to move. The instrument of poetry was the rhetorical example.[9]

In England, Clark shows, Sidney and Ben Jonson follow this view. We have seen it in detail in Milton.

[8] Columbia *Milton*, III, Pt. I, 303.
[9] Donald L. Clark, *Rhetoric and Poetry in the Renaissance* (New York, Columbia University Press, 1922), p. 138.

In *Paradise Lost,* then, the story of man's fall, its causes and consequences, is an example from which readers are expected to arrive by induction at certain conclusions. Therefore, if *Paradise Lost* is considered an argument as well as an epic (and lines 25 and 26 of Book I assert it to be an argument) an analysis of the narrative becomes an analysis of that example.

The reader's task in following the argument is not a simple one, for he must share some of the difficulties that Milton faced as a writer. The complexity of *Paradise Lost* and the demands that it makes upon the attention of the reader are in part due to Milton's manifold aim. As a philosophical poet his task was to invent or to adapt (which is also invention) a story that would represent the world as he saw it or that would interpret or explain that aspect of it with which he was concerned. We may take Milton to mean this when he implies his resolution to write a doctrinal poem. As a moral poet, Milton had to present a narrative that would persuade his reader to adopt a scheme of life. This too, in so far as it is a matter of precept, we may take to be a "doctrinal" aim. But we have found the preceptive to be the lesser part of a poetic moral argument. It is the example that is most persuasive. It is of this that Milton thinks when he speaks of a poem "exemplary to a nation." His problem as a Christian poet, of course, was to keep in his invention within the framework set by revelation and tradition.

What we may call Milton's "metaphorical" view of Scripture and his consequent metaphorical treatment of transcendental material in *Paradise Lost* is of great assistance to him in the manipulation of his story, which still remains rigid enough to present poetic problems of the first magnitude. In response to Adam's request for news of what has passed in Heaven, Raphael prefaces his story with the following reservation:

> High matter thou injoinst me, O prime of men,
> Sad task and hard, for how shall I relate

To human sense th' invisible exploits
Of warring Spirits; how without remorse
The ruin of so many glorious once
And perfet while they stood; how last unfould
The secrets of another world, perhaps
Not lawful to reveal? yet for thy good
This is dispenc't, and what surmounts the reach
Of human sense, I shall delineate so,
By lik'ning spiritual to corporal forms,
As may express them best, though what if Earth
Be but the shaddow of Heav'n, and things therein
Each to other like, more then on earth is thought?

(V, 563–576)

This passage, surely, is a direction to Adam designed to guide
him in the interpretation of Raphael's story. It is a direction to
us in reading the poem. Hanford says of the passage that it contains

The philosophic assumption which underlies the narrative and indeed Milton's whole conception of his poem. . . . Spiritual facts can
only so be represented to human sense, but there is also perhaps a real
analogy between earth and Heaven, the former being, according to the
Platonic doctrine of ideas, an imperfect replica of the latter, and this
analogy justifies the phrasing of divine events in material terms.[10]

There is an illuminating parallel in the *Christian Doctrine,* on
the interpretation of Scripture:

Our safest way is to form in our minds such a conception of God, as
shall correspond with his own delineation and representation of himself in the sacred writings. For granting that both in the literal and
figurative descriptions of God, he is exhibited not as he really is, but
in such manner as may be within the scope of our comprehensions, yet
we ought to entertain such a conception of him, as he, in condescending

[10] James Holly Hanford, *A Milton Handbook* (3d. ed., New York,
F. S. Crofts and Co., 1939), p. 205. Reprinted by permission of the publishers.

to accommodate himself to our capacities, has shown that he desires we should conceive. For it is on this very account that he has lowered himself to our level, lest in our flights above the reach of human understanding, and beyond the written word of Scripture, we should be tempted to indulge in vague cogitations and subtleties.[11]

Scripture itself, then, for Milton, is figurative, almost metaphorical, in its method, especially in its revelation of God. But the metaphor is as near to literal truth of the mysteries involved as human understanding can come and therefore must be interpreted not at all by human minds, but rather must be accepted literally. When Raphael tells Adam of heavenly events, of angelic motives and of heavenly war, Adam is to believe literally what is not literally true but is as near the truth as his limited understanding can come. So too perhaps the reader—not only of Raphael's narrative, but of the whole. If the correspondence between Heaven and Earth is as close as lines 574–576 of Book V suggest, we shall come closer to literal truth than it may seem at first.

Milton presents his narrative and his ethic in conventional Christian terms, however heterodox and eclectic he may be in his theology. To read *Paradise Lost* with appreciation and understanding, those readers of the poem who have been deprived by twentieth-century doubts and denials of the privilege of reading it with a faith comparable to its author's must accept the story as they accept Homeric fable. Whether we believe in a family of gods on Olympus or not, we must accept them as agents in Homer's story. Whether we believe as Milton does, or whether we do not, in the interference in the affairs of men of a personal God, his Son, his angels, and his enemies, we must accept them as agents in Milton's story. "The poem no longer has for us," writes Sir Herbert Grierson, "the appeal it possessed for those who saw in it, as the Greeks saw in the *Iliad,* a chapter of his-

[11] Columbia *Milton,* XIV, 31–33.

tory." [12] Perhaps not. But our knowledge of astronomy does not interfere with our acceptance of Milton's use of the Ptolemaic system; indeed, his own knowledge of astronomy did not. Our knowledge of geology need not interfere with his account of creation. Surely then twentieth-century ignorance of God and of angels need not interfere with our acceptance of Milton's use of them. The poem may even help dispel some of that ignorance.

"Yet we are not so far rid of that feeling" (that the story is a chapter of history), Grierson continues, that we can contemplate *Paradise Lost* "without some disposition to challenge the theological positions, its central justification of God's ways to men." We have seen in our brief survey of Milton's theory of poetry that Milton accepts the ethical principle that the end of knowledge is virtuous action. Whether we challenge the theological position or not, we can learn what Milton's conception of virtuous action is, what the problem and what the obligation of the human individual is, what the reward for perseverance and what the penalty for failure, what the means and what the dangers —all these we may learn and formulate, for all these Milton has undertaken "with a solid and treatable smoothness to paint out and describe." The twentieth-century reader who rejects the detail of the theology may or may not reject the ethic.

An exposition of a poem designedly theological can hardly avoid treating theological problems. If the poem is concerned with the relationship between God and man, the exposition must concern itself with that relationship. Ours will do so with an informality that reflects both the writer's incapacity to deal formally with theological problems and his conviction that *Paradise Lost* is a "feigned example," a fiction, however historical and however philosophical, and that its meaning may therefore be

[12] *Milton and Wordsworth: Poets and Prophets* (Cambridge, England, Cambridge University Press; New York, The Macmillan Company, 1937), p. 95. Reprinted by permission of the publishers.

understood and its bearing on conduct determined without special concern for theological controversies. Our concern will be to determine what according to Milton should be the guiding principles of an individual human life. If the end of *Paradise Lost* is virtuous action, what guides to such action does it offer? In the analysis of *Paradise Lost* as an argument, the answer to this question will be our chief concern.

But we must not forget that to the extent to which one makes allowances for Milton's misfortune in being a Christian in a Christian age and country, one departs from Milton's meaning and falls into the not uncommon error of speculating about what Milton would have thought if he had not thought what he did. The moral principles that we can isolate from Milton's theology were not enough for Milton. They had validity for him only within the framework of his theology. To remove Milton's ethical system from that framework is to separate it from the basis of its validity.

Two Rhetorical Aids
to Proof

T HE POET who accepts persuasion as his end employs various devices of rhetoric in order to achieve it. The analysis of these devices will throw light on his meaning. In particular, as part of the technique of persuasion, Milton sought by his prologues to secure the confidence of his audience and by his narrative to engage their affections.

It was Milton's habit in his controversial prose to write frequently and at length about himself.[1] This habit has been cited often enough as proof of his arrogance, his pride, his self-concern. There is a great deal of self-concern, and some arrogance, in Milton. But if he liked to write of himself, he made good use of the liking—a use which he explains among other places in the *Apology for Smectymnuus:*

. . . I conceav'd my selfe to be now not as mine own person, but as a member incorporate into that truth whereof I was perswaded, and whereof I had declar'd openly to be a partaker. Whereupon I thought it my duty, if not to my selfe, yet to the religious cause I had in hand, not to leave on my garment the least spot, or blemish in good name so long as God should give me to say that which might wipe it off.[2]

[1] This discussion is a redaction of my article, "The Function of the Prologues in *Paradise Lost*," *PMLA*, LVII (1942), 697–704; reprinted by permission of the publishers.

[2] Columbia *Milton*, III, Pt. I, 284.

He explains it again:

... since I dare not wish to passe this life unpersecuted of slanderous tongues, for God hath told us that to be generally prais'd is wofull, I shall relye on his promise to free the innocent from causeless aspersions: whereof nothing sooner can assure me, then if I shall feele him now assisting me in the just vindication of my selfe, which yet I could deferre, it being more meet that to those other matters of publick debatement in this book I should give attendance first, but that I feare it would but harme the truth, for me to reason in her behalfe, so long as I should suffer my honest estimation to lye unpurg'd from these insolent suspicions.[3]

This explanation, which Milton repeats explicitly or by implication many times in the course of his voluminous controversy, should be taken seriously. Certainly it is good rhetoric, and as such it gives us a basis upon which to judge the "autobiographical digressions," as they have been called—at least a basis on which to ask whether the autobiographical and self-laudatory passages are digressions at all. For what Milton is saying is that they are not digressions, but part of the machinery of persuasion. "All the most distinguished teachers of rhetoric," Milton tells his fellow-students in the first of his Prolusions, at Cambridge,

have left behind the opinion ... that in every kind of speaking, whether demonstrative or deliberative or judicial, the exordium ought to be occupied with securing the goodwill of the listeners; otherwise the minds of the audience could not be persuaded nor could the cause be triumphant as one might wish.[4]

This is familiar doctrine too. "It is not true," says Aristotle,

... that the personal goodness revealed by the speaker contributes nothing to his power of persuasion; on the contrary, his character may almost be called the most effective means of persuasion he possesses.[5]

The point makes itself. Like the address to Parliament at the beginning of *Areopagitica* and that other at the beginning of the

---

[3] *Ibid.*, pp. 296–297.   [4] *Ibid.*, XII, 119.   [5] *Rhetorica*, i. 2.

Likeliest Means to Remove Hirelings out of the Church, where
flattery of Parliament is subtly blended with a reminder of past
services to Parliament, these "digressions" of autobiography, self-
congratulation, and self-praise are designed to secure the attention and approbation of the audience by demonstrating the probity
of the writer. As such, whether successful or not, they are an
important means of persuasion. If they are inserted from impulse, if they are sprung from Milton's pride, and whether ad-
visedly or not, there are good rhetorical reasons for them as well.

That this is good rhetoric, as well as traditional rhetoric, is
obvious. Surely the speaker who can secure the goodwill of his
audience and demonstrate his own fitness to speak on the subject
in hand has taken his audience half way to persuasion. To Milton
it is more than a mere matter of technique, however. Milton
accepts Quintilian's definition of the orator as "A good man
skilled in speaking," saying (again in the *Apology for Smectymnuus*) that

doubtlesse that indeed according to art is most eloquent, which returnes
and approaches neerest to nature from whence it came; and they
expresse nature best, who in their lives least wander from her safe leading, which may be call'd regenerate reason. So that how he should be
truly eloquent who is not withall a good man, I see not.[6]

Elsewhere Milton observes that "he who would write of worthy
deeds worthily must write with mental endowments and experience of affairs not less than were in the doer of the same." [7] If
Milton is to achieve true eloquence, then, to speak with the sub-
stance as well as the semblance of worth,[8] he must himself be

---

[6] Columbia *Milton,* III, Pt. I, 287.
[7] In a letter to Henry DeBrass, Columbia *Milton,* XII, 93.
[8] The parallel with the description of Satan's eloquence (I, 529) is
obvious. The falsity of the speeches of the rebel angels is more than
rhetorical in any narrow sense of the word. Their evil counsel springs
from their own evil. Not even Beelzebub is evil enough to father the

good. If he is to be believed, he must demonstrate his goodness. Although the establishment of his character is a matter of rhetorical technique, necessary if readers are to be persuaded and the cause be triumphant as one might wish, the need that it be established is philosophic as well as rhetorical.

If so high a standard is set for the orator, no less can be set for the poet. The conception of the poet held by certain critics of the Renaissance, including Milton, we have seen, is another borrowing of poetic from rhetorical theory. We return to the famous description of the noble poet in the *Apology for Smectymnuus:*

> . . . he who would not be frustrate of his hope to write well hereafter in laudable things, ought him selfe to be a true Poem, that is, a composition, and patterne of the best and honourablest things.[9]

Since for Milton persuasion is an end of poetry as well as of oratory, all the rhetorical and philosophical reasons that justify including affirmations of his own probity in his prose pamphlets apply to *Paradise Lost* as well. If Milton is to be successful in his assertion of Providence, in his justification of God, and in his larger intention to lead men into paths of honesty and the good life, he must convince his readers of his probity and of his right and authority to speak on the subject in hand.

------

plan adopted in the council of the second book. It comes from Satan,

> for whence,
> But from the Author of all ill could Spring
> So deep a malice?

(II, 380–382.)

[9] Columbia *Milton,* III, Pt. I, 303. Ida Langdon, in *Milton's Theory of Poetry and Fine Art* (New Haven, 1924), pp. 174–175, brings together, as background for this opinion, passages from Strabo and Longinus and ancients less explicit than they, and cites Ben Jonson to show its currency in the English Renaissance. In the Italian Renaissance we may find it in Minturno's definition of the poet as a "good man skilled in speech and imitation." See, also, Clark, *Rhetoric and Poetry in the Renaissance,* p. 137.

Paradise Lost is an epic before it is an argument. Its essential structure is determined by epic principles and is less flexible than the structure of a political pamphlet—or even than a formal oration like *Areopagitica*. We should not expect, therefore, to find in it such generous portions of self-praise as we find in the prose, nor to find it in the same tone. We do not indeed find it by any means so obvious, for with characteristic ingenuity, Milton has adapted to this rhetorical purpose a time-honored epic convention —the invocation.

E. M. W. Tillyard has pointed out that the invocations to Books I, III, VII, and IX of *Paradise Lost* are not "superfluities too beautiful to be spared," but are instead clear marks of the stages of the story, indications of the shifting point of view.[10] They also serve the rhetorical function we have indicated, as Tillyard suggests when he observes that "It is natural that Milton, believing in the high seriousness of his purpose, should invoke the Holy Spirit to be his help." [11] The appeal for divine guidance is an implied claim that divine guidance has been granted.[12] Later, of course, Milton makes the claim explicit, identifying the Muse of Book I with Urania, who has been his constant aid.

On any subject, but on a religious subject especially, he can make no higher claim to authority. The claim is made formally when in Book I, line 34, the Muse (in good epic tradition) responds to Milton's direct question. Since the question is about

[10] E. M. W. Tillyard *Milton* (London, Chatto and Windus; New York, Dial Press, 1930), pp. 237–256. These passages are reprinted by permission of the publishers.

[11] *Ibid.*, p. 245.

[12] The claim of divine guidance is a common one in the prose, where it is also a means of persuasion. Even in the *Doctrine and Discipline of Divorce* Milton claims it, arguing that it cannot be explained on any other principle that two champions of "domestic freedom" (himself and Martin Bucer) should have been independently raised up for the instruction of Englishmen.

Satan and directed to a Muse from whose view nothing is hidden by Heaven nor the deep Tract of Hell, Milton has claimed divine authority (in lines 1 to 25) to justify God's ways, and (in lines 26 to 34) explicitly to speak of Hell. He has indeed written a prologue at once to the whole poem and to the first movement, and he has established himself as fit to speak. The exordium is occupied with securing the good will of the listeners.

The invocations to Books III, VII, and IX serve similar dual functions.[13] In Book III, where (as Tillyard observes) the scene shifts, the argument shifts also, with an advance in the logical proof. The demonstration of Satan's evil has been well begun; the demonstration of God's goodness is now to be undertaken. The invocation to light, fitting for the shift in setting that accompanies Satan's journey to the realms of light, is fitting also to Milton's plan of allowing God to justify himself in his own words.

---

[13] For us, as for Tillyard, the brief prologue to Book IV is different not only in length but in kind also. As a narrative device its function is clear. It serves as prologue not only to Book IV, in which the scope of the narrative is broadened to include Earth, it serves also as prologue to the following books, and as narrative foreshadowing. In its cry for

> that warning voice, which he who saw
> Th' *Apocalyps,* heard cry in Heaven aloud,
>   . . . that now,
> While time was, our first-Parents had bin warnd

it points clearly to the passage in Book V where God "fulfills all justice" by sending his messenger, Raphael, to provide the "warning voice" that should have enabled them to "scape the mortal snare." But this prologue is not an invocation. It is not part of the poet's justification of himself as qualified to speak. Except as it calls attention to the special warning given Adam and Eve after Eve's dream (an important part of the vindication) and is hence a part of the proof, it is not persuasion at all. Its chief function is narrative. It neither seeks nor claims divine guidance, as do the various invocations. The claims of special fitness implicit and explicit in the first lines of Book I and of Book III must carry until Book VII.

> Taught by the heav'nly Muse to venture down
> The dark descent, and up to reascend,
>
> (III, 19–20)

Milton now revisits light, expressing the hope and the belief that Celestial light will

> Shine inward, and the mind through all her powers ·
> Irradiate,
>
> (III, 52–53)

"wisdome at one entrance quite shut out," in order that he

> may see and tell
> Of things invisible to mortal sight.
>
> (III, 54–55)

Here guidance in the two books accomplished is claimed specifically. The claim to future inspiration is by implication only, but it is clearly intended.

In the prologue to Book VII the claim of past inspiration is again explicit and the appeal for further aid is repeated:

> Up led by thee
> Into the Heav'n of Heav'ns I have presum'd,
> An Earthlie Guest, and drawn Empyreal Aire,
> Thy tempring; with like safetie guided down
> Return me to my Native Element.
>
> (VII, 12–16)

But if I have succeeded thus far, Milton adds in effect, and have shown myself capable of writing of Heaven and Hell, for what remains I am surely adequate, counting still upon the assistance of the Muse:

> Half yet remaines unsung, but narrower bound
> Within the visible Diurnal Spheare;

Standing on Earth, not rapt above the Pole,
More safe I Sing with mortal voice, unchang'd
To hoarce or mute, though fall'n on evil dayes,
On evil dayes though fall'n, and evil tongues;
In darkness, and with dangers compast round,
And solitude; yet not alone, while thou
Visit'st my slumbers Nightly, or when Morn
Purples the East: still govern thou my Song,
Urania, and fit audience find, though few.

                                        (VII, 21–31)

The prologue to Book IX, like the brief introduction to Book IV, is different in kind from those to Books I, III, and VII. It is not an invocation, a prayer for guidance, but primarily a defense of the subject of *Paradise Lost* as

                                        argument
Not less but more Heroic than the wrauth
Of stern *Achilles.*

                                        (IX, 13–15)

Here, instead of a petition that she come, we have the final positive claim of inspiration from a Muse who does come, "unimplor'd." Even Milton's doubts that "an age too late, or cold/ Climat, or Years" may damp his intended wing enable him to reaffirm his possession of supernatural aid. Similarly his admitted unwillingness and unfitness to write of conventional heroic subjects,

                Not sedulous by Nature to indite
                Warrs, hitherto the onely Argument
                Heroic deem'd,

                                        (IX, 27–29)

leads him to assert once more that to him

                                        of these
                Nor skilld nor studious, higher Argument

Remaines, sufficient of it self to raise
That name,

(IX, 41–44)

and to affirm his fitness for that higher. It is the final instance of his direct claim to authority. As it marks the narrative shift, so it marks also a new part of the argument: man's fall, the motives for it, the justice of his doom, and the mercy of his salvation from it.

Each of the four great prologues, then, has not only the narrative function that Tillyard assigns to them, but rhetorical functions as well. Following his practice in the prose pamphlets, Milton in *Paradise Lost,* as a means of persuasion, makes the strongest of all possible claims to authority and probity and makes it at points in the argument where its very "interruption" serves to call the reader's attention to the logical as to the narrative structure of the poem.

It is not enough, we have found Aristotle saying, for an orator to establish in his audience an attitude toward himself. He must also establish an attitude toward his subject, arousing in his audience whatever emotion is appropriate to his cause.

Where an argument is to be advanced by narrative example, every character and every incident may be used for this rhetorical purpose. As the argument progresses towards the reader's conviction, the narrative enforces it by enlisting his sympathies and affections. This is true of all successful narrative, argumentative or not, to the extent to which the engagement of the sympathies and affections is necessary to secure and to retain the reader's interest in the story. Indeed, the narrator, where there is a conflict in his narrative, usually leads his reader to take sides. If there is a playgoer to whom the cause of King Claudius in *Hamlet* seems just, we may say that with that playgoer Shakespeare failed, just as he failed with him who dismisses Macbeth as a "bad man" and hence not capable of commanding sympathy. Or, of course, the actor or the playgoer has failed. Similarly it is the function of an orator to arouse in the reader the emotions that will lead to the judgment desired, his love for the protagonist, his hatred for the antagonist. "Of this man Pickwick," says Serjeant Buzfuz,

I will say little; the subject presents but few attractions; and I, gentlemen, am not the man, nor are you, gentlemen, the men, to delight in the contemplation of revolting heartlessness, and of systematic villainy.

"I am not the man," to be sure, is calculated to secure for Buzfuz the confidence of the jury; but "revolting heartlessness" and "systematic villainy" are calculated to rouse the jury to hatred of Pickwick by identifying him with hateful things. Both are important to Serjeant Buzfuz' argument.

When the aim is both narrative and argumentative, the devices that determine the reader's attitude toward the characters involved serve both purposes. Serjeant Buzfuz' argument succeeds with the jury where it does not with the reader not only because the reader knows the facts and the jury doesn't, but also because Dickens has long since enlisted the affections of the reader for Mr. Pickwick and assured his antagonism, if not to Mrs. Bardell, at least to Messrs. Dodson and Fogg. The arguments of Buzfuz and Dickens are directed to different audiences. Among the members of the smaller jury the advantage is with Buzfuz; among those of the larger it is with Dickens.

As with Dickens, so with Milton. Every means by which character is presented in *Paradise Lost* we may say serves the argument as well as the narrative. As we presented the alternative for *Macbeth* and *Hamlet,* so may we for *Paradise Lost.* If the reader's sympathies are with Satan, Milton has failed. Or the reader has failed.

The most obvious device to arouse emotions in forensic oratory is name-calling. Serjeant Buzfuz calls Mr. Pickwick a Being, a monster, a serpent, a sapper and miner, a slow coach, and a ruthless destroyer, leaving no doubt in the minds of jurymen as to their proper feelings. Mrs. Bardell, on the contrary, is a "lonely and desolate widow," a "sensitive and confiding female." As this is aimed at the feelings of the jury, so *Paradise Lost* also contains much of the same kind of appeal to our feelings. But the attribution (true or false) of good or evil deeds is still more telling. "Systematic villainy" is the phrase that leads Mr. Pickwick to protest.

In *Paradise Lost* the success of the proof depends upon the demonstration of the evil of Satan, the innocence and subsequent guilt of Adam and Eve, the justice of God, and the compassion of the Son. These demonstrated, the reader's emotions will take care of themselves. There are also more direct attempts to arouse the proper emotions toward the several characters in their various situations. In our examination of it, we must guard against the danger of taking the word of one character about another:

. . . we must not regard the poet's words as his own, but consider who it is that speaks in the play, and what the person says; for different persons are introduced, sometimes good, sometimes bad, sometimes wise men, sometimes fools, and they speak not always the poet's own opinion, but what is most fitting to each character.[14]

We must be sure it is Milton speaking in his own person or else be careful to make the proper allowance for the speaker. It is folly to take Satan's estimate of God (although it has been done) or to think of God with Eve as "the Great Forbidder." That is to take the word of Serjeant Buzfuz over the word of Dickens. With these cautions in mind, it will be enough to look briefly at the treatment afforded by Milton to Adam, Eve, God, and Satan.

The obvious place to look for epithets or descriptions designed to determine the reader's attitude toward a given agent is at that point in the narrative at which the agent is introduced—in the

[14] *First Defence,* Columbia *Milton,* VII, 307.

case of Adam and Eve, in the fourth book. They have already been mentioned at the beginning of Book I as "our Grand Parents," and Eve as "The Mother of Mankind." At the beginning of Book IV they are called "our first-Parents" and "innocent frail man." Here the context is as telling as the language, for the passage is that in which Milton seeks the warning voice of St. John,

> that now,
> While time was, our first-Parents had bin warnd
> The coming of thir secret foe, and scap'd
> Haply so scap'd his mortal snare; for now
> *Satan,* now first inflam'd with rage, came down,
> The Tempter ere th'Accuser of man-kind,
> To wreck on innocent frail man his loss
> Of that first Battel, and his flight to Hell.
>
> (IV, 5–12)

There is not much question here to whom Milton wishes us to be partisan. Nor is there when

> the Fiend
> Saw undelighted all delight, all kind
> Of living Creatures new to sight and strange:
> Two of far nobler shape erect and tall,
> Godlike erect, with native Honour clad
> In naked Majestie seemd Lords of all,
> And worthie seemd, for in thir looks Divine
> The image of thir glorious Maker shon,
> Truth, wisdome, Sanctitude severe and pure,
> Severe but in true filial freedom plac't.
>
> (IV, 285–294)

It is well to recall that this is not only Satan's first view of our Grand Parents; it is our first view as well. The passage is therefore worth quoting at greater length, for the description is made still more specific and still more appealing:

> For contemplation hee and valour formd,
> For softness shee and sweet attractive Grace,
> Hee for God only, shee for God in him:
> His fair large Front and Eye sublime declar'd
> Absolute rule; and Hyacynthin Locks
> Round from his parted forelock manly hung
> Clustring, but not beneath his shoulders broad:
> Shee as a vail down to the slender waste
> Her unadorned golden tresses wore
> Dissheveld, but in wanton ringlets wav'd
> As the Vine curles her tendrils, which impli'd
> Subjection, but requir'd with gentle sway,
> And by her yielded, by him best received,
> Yielded with coy submission, modest pride,
> And sweet reluctant amorous delay.
>
> (IV, 297–311)

By the appearance of Adam and Eve thus presented, and by the life of tranquil innocence that they lead, even Satan is moved. How can we fail to be moved with him?

As Adam and Eve are very briefly commended to us at the beginning of Book I, concerned chiefly with Satan, so also is God, who is referred to as "their Creator," "the most High," "the Almighty Power," and as "Eternal Justice." But God and the Son are not directly presented to us until Book III. Again it is well to quote:

> Now had the Almighty Father from above,
> From the pure Empyrean where he sits
> High Thron'd above all highth, bent down his eye
> His own works and their works at once to view:

About him all the Sanctities of Heaven
Stood thick as Starrs, and from his sight receiv'd
Beatitude past utterance; on his right
The radiant image of his Glory sat,
His onely Son.

(III, 56–64)

For dramatic as well as theological reasons, of course, God's awful glory is presented to us here as elsewhere by indirection, in the "Beatitude past utterance" received from his presence by the heavenly host and through his radiant image in his Son. When God speaks, as we shall see, Milton's intent becomes still clearer.

Satan is presented in the first book and again and again throughout, so that the reader feels himself better acquainted with Satan than with any of the other agents—and nearer akin to him. Because of this kinship, and because of this acquaintance, some readers are misled into sympathy with Satan. Before the fall, the purity of Adam and Eve is unmixed; and the glory of God is unmixed. The evil of Satan is also unmixed. But Satan, evil as he is, is built on a grand scale and, for purposes of the narrative and of the proof, must be. Without great powers he can be no adversary even for Adam and Eve. The grandeur of Satan has led some who do not admire God into admiration of the devil.

There is no obscurity, however, when we are first introduced to Satan in Book I. There we find epithets enough inviting us to share Milton's rage at "Th'infernal Serpent." When the Muse responds to the direct question of the first invocation, it is to say that it was Satan, stirred up with envy and revenge, who deceived the Mother of Mankind and seduced our first parents to a foul revolt (*envy, revenge, deceived, seduced,* and *foul revolt* are all Milton's words), having first raised *impious* war in Heaven. Satan we first see "rowling" in the fiery gulf. His baleful eyes, as he looks about him, give evidence of affliction and dismay, to be sure, but "mixt with obdurate pride and steadfast hate." Having taken his bearings, Satan sees beside him one *next in crime,* to whom he utters the first words we hear from him.

So far, surely, we have been told by Milton's idiom what to expect. Satan has been called the *Infernal Serpent,* and the *Arch-enemy* (as well as *Satan,* which is as bad a name as either). He has been accused of envy, revengefulness, pride, hate, deceit, impiety, and rebellion, and he has been seen "rowling" in a fiery gulf prepared for him by Eternal Justice, so named. We have also been told what feelings are proper in us toward Adam, Eve, and God.

The descriptions of Adam, Eve, God, the Son, and Satan are but the least of the means by which our emotions are involved in the poem. The words and deeds of these agents have much greater effect. This effect is cumulative. Since it is the formal argument of the poem with which we are concerned primarily, and since that argument is coextensive with and inseparable from the narrative, which is the example, the full exposition of the appeal to the emotions is a mere by-product of the analysis of the logical proof. If it is necessary to the logical proof to demonstrate the evil of Satan, the demonstration itself is an appeal to our emotions—if men still hate evil. Those who do not will not be persuaded.

CHAPTER III

The Evil of Satan

U NDERTAKING to justify God's ways to men, Milton must deal with the paradox of evil. Whence, in a world governed by a beneficent deity, does evil come? Its introduction into the world of men is his subject. "For Milton with the beliefs he professed," says Tillyard,

the Fall was necessarily the most pregnant event in the history of the world. The only event that could seriously compete with it was the entrance of sin into Heaven, but the direct effect of this was limited to expulsion and irrevocable condemnation: there was no evocation of grace.[1]

The introduction of sin into Heaven, which is the entrance of evil into the universe, Milton explains in the manner of Plato dealing with insolubles, by myth—in the story of the birth of Sin, sprung from the brow of Satan. Evil is thus self-generated in Satan, although by God's permissive will. There is no further explanation, for how an angel falls into sin is a mystery. To seek to know is to commit the sin of Eve, seeking knowledge that can be God's alone.

But Milton is writing to justify his God to mankind; and the important question, not only because the fall of man evokes God's grace but also because it is personal to men, is how evil came to Earth, not how it came to Heaven. Again, of course, by God's permissive (not his constitutive) will. The active will in this matter is Satan's. Milton undertakes to prove that Satan is

---

[1] *Milton* (London, Chatto and Windus; New York, Dial Press, 1930), p. 257. Reprinted by permission of the publishers.

responsible for the introduction of evil into the world and that he is hateful because he is evil.

It is strange to have to prove the devil bad. But we have seen Milton begin the proof by calling the devil names, and he completes the task. In spite of Milton's care in the matter, however, some readers of Milton have thought he cherished a more or less secret admiration for Satan. Some have argued that he projected himself into Satan to a greater extent than into other characters. Some have found in Milton's Satan a self-portrait—a wishful self-portrait. Some, mistaking for virtue Satan's magnificent energy and his royal pride, or being themselves of his party, have found Satan an admirable figure. This is to say that Milton did not know what he was talking about.

The literary heretics who have thought Satan the central figure in *Paradise Lost,* who have regarded him as a thoroughly admirable moral agent, and who have thought that Milton consciously or unconsciously, more or less, identified himself with Satan, have been classified together under the label *Satanists.* Among professional Miltonists they are not now very many. But orthodoxy is to be expected among the ordained, and there are still many nonprofessional dissenters. However frequently it may have been done of late, to insist upon the evil of Satan in *Paradise Lost* is not quite to belabor a dead horse. We have two reasons for doing it: first, not to drive hirelings out of the true church, but rather to bring the unpaid clergy into it; second, to follow Milton in the emphasis which he puts upon the matter in *Paradise Lost.* He treats it at length and with care.

At the argument of the Satanists we need look but briefly, taking a statement of the case from Shelley, who was sure enough of his judgment to express it twice, in almost identical language:

Nothing can exceed the energy and magnificence of the character of Satan as expressed in *Paradise Lost.* It is a mistake to suppose that he could ever have been intended for the popular personification of evil. Implacable hate, patient cunning, and a sleepless refinement of device to inflict the extremest anguish on an enemy, these things are evil; and, although venial in a slave, are not to be forgiven in a tyrant; although redeemed by much that ennobles his defeat in one subdued, are marked by all that dishonours his conquest in the victor. Milton's Devil as a moral being is as far superior to his God, as one who perseveres in some purpose which he has conceived to be excellent in spite of adversity and torture, is to one who in the cold security of undoubted triumph inflicts the most horrible revenge upon his enemy, not from any mistaken notion of inducing him to repent of a perseverance in enmity, but with the alleged design of exasperating him to new torments. Milton has so far violated the popular creed (if this shall be judged to be a violation) as to have alleged no superiority of moral virtue to his god over his devil. And this bold neglect of a direct moral purpose is the most decisive proof of the supremacy of Milton's genius.[2]

If this is eloquent, it is eloquent nonsense.

The judgment of the character of God involved in Shelley's

[2] *A Defence of Poetry,* in *Works of Percy Bysshe Shelley,* ed. Harry Buxton Forman (8 vols., London, 1880), VII, 127–128. In his essay "On the Devil, and Devils," prepared for publication in 1839 but withdrawn, Shelley writes as follows (*Works,* VI, 388–389):

"Nothing can exceed the grandeur and the energy of the character of the Devil, as expressed in Paradise Lost. He is a Devil, very different from the popular personification of evil, and it is a mistake to suppose that he was intended for an idealism of Evil. Malignity, implacable hate, cunning, and refinement of device to inflict the utmost anguish on an enemy, these, which are venial in a slave, are not to be forgiven in a tyrant; these, which are redeemed by much that ennobles in one subdued, are marked by all that dishonours his conquest in the victor. Milton's Devil, as a moral being, is as far superior to his God, as one who perseveres in a purpose which he has conceived to be excellent, in spite of adversity and torture, is to one who in the cold security of undoubted triumph inflicts the most horrible revenge upon his enemy—not from any mistaken notion of bringing him to repent of a perseverance in enmity, but with the open and alleged design of exasperating him to deserve new torments.

". . . Thus much is certain, that Milton gives the Devil all imaginable advantage; and the arguments with which he exposes the injustice and impotent weakness of his adversary, are such as, had they been printed, distinct from the shelter of any dramatic order, would have been answered by the most conclusive of syllogisms—persecution."

estimate of Satan we need not consider for the moment. Our question is whether *Paradise Lost,* in spite of the epithets Milton applies to Satan, presents Satan as the great moral agent Shelley describes. First of all, we must distinguish between Satan's character (his moral bent) and Satan as a character (as an agent in a story). His energy under either classification we shall hardly be inclined to question. Nor is there any question of the magnificence of Milton's conception of him. He is one of the great epic figures, one of the great creations in the world's literature. If "Satanists" were content to describe him so, we should have no quarrel.

The values upon which such a judgment must be based are "artistic," not "moral." Satan's is a convincing portrait, one that carries with it the illusion of reality. As an agent in *Paradise Lost* he performs that part of the action which the story imposes upon him without apparent inconsistency of character. As we believe in his character, so we also believe in what he thinks and says and does. If readers generally believe in him more fully than in God or in Adam, or in Eve; if, that is, he is generally more consistent, more believable, more clearly integrated and more completely realized, then we may agree that as a character he is Milton's greatest achievement in *Paradise Lost.* We may not be so positive of this as some, but it may be conceded without harm to the argument. Satan as an artistic creation is the best agent in the story. His actions accord with his *ethos.*

But Satan was a very bad angel, and Milton knew it.

Raphael demonstrates the evil of Satan to Adam by an account of the rebellion in Heaven. Of that we shall have something to say in a later chapter—enough to show the groundlessness of his rebellion. We as well as Adam hear Raphael's account of it and his judgment of Satan. But for us there is the additional evidence of Satan's conduct toward man. This is much more telling as argument than the account of the rebellion in Heaven, for in his attack upon Eve, Satan is attacking us. This, surely, is one of Milton's reasons for making that attack the central action. It begins, we may say, in *Paradise Lost,* with the speech to Beelzebub which is Satan's first utterance in the poem, a speech that gives us immediate insight into Satan's character:

> who knew
> The force of those dire Arms? yet not for those,
> Nor what the Potent Victor in his rage
> Can else inflict, do I repent or change,
> Though chang'd in outward lustre; that fixt mind
> And high disdain, from sence of injur'd merit,
> That with the mightiest rais'd me to contend,
> And to the fierce contention brought along
> Innumerable force of Spirits arm'd
> That durst dislike his reign, and me preferring,
> His utmost power with adverse power oppos'd
> In dubious Battel on the Plains of Heav'n,
> And shook his throne. What though the field be lost?
> All is not lost; the unconquerable Will,
> And study of revenge, immortal hate,
> And courage never to submit or yield:
> And what is else not to be overcome?
> That Glory never shall his wrath or might
> Extort from me. To bow and sue for grace
> With suppliant knee, and deifie his power
> Who from the terrour of this Arm so late
> Doubted his Empire, that were low indeed,
> That were an ignominy and shame beneath
> This downfall.
>
> (I, 93–116)

Now if obstinate refusal to repent of wrongs done, if disdain, and pride, and the study of revenge are noble qualities, and if to

"bow and sue for grace" to God, to admit His deity, is ignominy
and shame, then Satan does indeed reveal himself in this speech
to be of surpassing nobility. With this nobility the resolution
that follows is in keeping: "To wage by force or guile eternal
war." We have seen enough followers of Satan in our day re-
solved like him to wage by force or guile eternal war to make a
judgment of the virtue of their master.

"Of this be sure," Satan says to Beelzebub, rallying him from
his despair,

> of this be sure,
> To do ought good never will be our task,
> But ever to do ill our sole delight,
> As being the contrary to his high will
> Whom we resist. If then his Providence
> Out of our evil seek to bring forth good,
> Our labour must be to pervert that end,
> And out of good still to find means of evil;
> Which oft times may succeed, so as perhaps
> Shall grieve him, if I fail not, and disturb
> His inmost counsels from thir destind aim.
>
> (I, 158–168)

If we continue to take Shelley as spokesman for Satan's admirers,
we see at once where the difference between us lies, for Shelley
describes Satan's worth as the worth of one who "perseveres in
some purpose which he has conceived to be excellent in spite of
adversity and torture." Even if Satan were stupid enough to
think his end not evil, his persistence in it would not be good. The
ascription of worth is doubly false, however, first because it is
not enough for a moral agent to conceive his end as excellent—
it must be excellent—and second because Satan does not so conceive his end. Evil is his good, to do ill his sole delight, not because by some paradox of word or thought evil is to him really
good, but because it is contrary to the will of his enemy, and so

perhaps will grieve him. A basic conflict is thus clearly stated. Anticipating God's providence, God's intention to bring good from evil, Satan resolves to "pervert that end,/ And out of good still to find means of evil."

Strength of body and mind, perseverance, intelligence, energy, eloquence—all these are good in the abstract, even admirable. Surely they are qualities it is well to have. But they are not virtue, and serve only to make ill-will more evil, as they make good-will the better, by implementing it.

Satan stands convicted by his own words. By further words too, of course, and by the words of his followers. During the debate over which Satan presides in Hell the demonstration of his personal evil is somewhat in abeyance while that of his followers is shown, until at last Beelzebub outlines the plan (already hinted at by Satan) of attacking God through man, a devilish counsel, and clearly not original to Beelzebub,

> for whence,
> But from the Author of all ill could Spring
> So deep a malice, to confound the race
> Of mankind in one root, and Earth with Hell
> To mingle and involve, done all to spite
> The great Creatour?
>
> (II, 380–385)

Whence indeed! For—save envy, of course, which springs not from man's enmity to them but from themselves—Satan and his crew have no basis for enmity to man. Nor do they feel enmity to man at first, and Satan for a moment even pities him. But man is favored of God. Injury to him is pain if not injury to God, Satan thinks; moreover, injury to man, weak and helpless as he is, in order merely to spite God, is the end that Satan conceives to be excellent, if we are to take Shelley's interpretation.

At the end of the "great consult" in Book II, Satan's part in the central action of *Paradise Lost,* his attack on God through man, has been planned and to that extent begun. It must now be executed; Satan is now to translate his evil thoughts and evil words into evil action. This he cannot do without an accompanying inner struggle which we can follow in his soliloquies. In them we shall find Satan judging himself in explicit terms. In three great soliloquies, that preceding the attempt on Eve in Book IV and those preceding the second attempt in Book IX, we find Satan's self-analysis leading to a clear statement of his motives. These passages are especially important to our argument not only for their content, but also because of their authority. It is in soliloquy alone that we may believe the Father of Lies and be sure of ourselves. This we may do on double grounds, first because self-accusation is trustworthy, and second because of the universally accepted literary convention that characters speak truth in soliloquy, that soliloquy is not used to deceive an audience. If under the restrictions of this convention Satan can find no pardon for himself, how can we pardon him?

At the beginning of the soliloquy in Book IV, we have a statement of the motives—"Pride and worse Ambition"—for the past action, specifically for Satan's rebellion. Pride a sin, and ambition worse because it leads to rebellious action as well as to rebellious thoughts. The Angel Raphael later confirms this judgment (as does indeed the whole narrative of the rebellion in Heaven) when he speaks of

> the deep fall
> Of those too high aspiring, who rebelld
> With *Satan.*
>
> (VI, 898–900)

An admission by Satan that the rebellion was guilty and groundless follows his own statement of motive immediately. It is groundless because Satan is God's creature:

> Ah wherefore! he deservd no such return
> From me, whom he created what I was
> In that bright eminence.
>
> (IV, 42–44)

This admission on Satan's part that he is God's creature is also important, for his denial of such creation in answer to Abdiel is part of his argument to foment rebellion in Heaven. The admission of the present soliloquy brands the claim a lie when we meet it chronologically earlier although actually later in the poem. We should have no such certain test of its truth if the narrative order did not differ from the chronological.

Satan's rebellion is groundless also, again on his own admission, because God's treatment of his creatures was good:

> Nor was his service hard.
> What could be less then to afford him praise,
> The easiest recompence, and pay him thanks,
> How due!
>
> (IV, 45–48)

Even the burden of gratitude Satan admits to have been illusory, unreal, rising simply from his own lack of it:

> Forgetful what from him I still receivd,
> And understood not that a grateful mind
> By owing owes not, but still pays, at once
> Indebted and dischargd; what burden then?
>
> (IV, 54–57)

Escape from self-conviction blocked in that direction, Satan turns to the very magnitude of God's gifts to him as an individual, basing his temptation upon his own exalted position in the hierarchy of Heaven.

> O had his powerful Destiny ordaind
> Me some inferiour Angel, I had stood

Then happie; no unbounded hope had rais'd
Ambition.
(IV, 58–61)

But this escape is denied him too. Since he was followed in his
own fall by his inferiors, he might (inferior himself) have followed some other power as great, like himself aspiring. Besides,

other Powers as great
Fell not, but stand unshak'n, from within
Or from without, to all temptations arm'd.
(IV, 63–65)

Thus he is brought inevitably to the ultimate question of responsibility, addressing it to himself: "Hadst thou the same free Will
and Power to stand?" The answer is immediate:

Thou hadst: whom hast thou then or what to accuse,
But Heav'ns free Love dealt equally to all?
Be then his Love accurst, since love or hate,
To me alike, it deals eternal woe.
Nay curs'd be thou; since against his thy will
Chose freely what it now so justly rues.
(IV, 67–72)

Satan is in the clutches of conscience and he is still intelligent.
This last passionate attempt at self-deception, therefore, must fail
like the others. There remains no hope but in repentance:

O then at last relent: is there no place
Left for Repentance, none for Pardon left?
(IV, 79–80)

That question also carries its own answer with it. Satan recognizes that pardon is possible only in terms of real repentance, by
submission, from which he is debarred by "disdain," by dread of
shame among the spirits who followed him in revolt, seduced

> With other promises and other vaunts
> Then to submit, boasting I could subdue
> Th' Omnipotent.

                                    (IV, 84–86)

In short he is debarred from submission by the continuing pride
that wrought his own rebellion. Realizing this, he no longer
attempts to throw the blame on God but bursts out in anguish at
his self-wrought lot:

> Ay me, they little know
> How dearly I abide that boast so vaine,
> Under what torments inwardly I groane;
> While they adore me on the Throne of Hell,
> With Diadem and Scepter high advanc'd
> The lower still I fall, onely Supream
> In miserie; such joy Ambition findes.

                                    (IV, 86–92)

Satan's despair is now inescapable. To it is added envy, and consequent to that the reaffirmation of his will to do evil:

> All hope excluded thus, behold in stead
> Of us out-cast, exil'd, his new delight,
> Mankind created, and for him this World.
> So farwel Hope, and with Hope farwel Fear,
> Farwel Remorse: all Good to me is lost;
> Evil be thou my Good; by thee at least
> Divided Empire with Heav'ns King I hold
> By thee, and more then half perhaps will reigne;
> As Man ere long, and this new World shall know.

                                    (IV, 105–113)

As the soliloquy we have been discussing precedes Satan's interrupted attempt on the sleeping Eve, so the temptation in Book IX
is preceded by soliloquies—soliloquies that show very clearly

Satan's further hardening in evil. In Book IX our first glimpse of him is of his return to Eden at midnight:

> now improv'd
> In meditated fraud and malice, bent
> On mans destruction, maugre what might hap
> Of heavier on himself.
>
> (IX, 54–57)

Here the phrase "meditated fraud and malice" shows us once more how deliberately Satan has chosen his course.

This is a changed Satan from that of Book IV. The change has often been noted. In Book IV Satan faced his own iniquity, admitting the goodness of God, admitting God's right to rule, and the benevolence of that rule. Here his character has so far disintegrated that no possibility of repentance occurs to him. Even here, however, Satan does not so far delude himself as to think that his cause is good, or that he can find satisfaction in success. He has said farewell to hope, to happiness:

> But neither here seek I, no nor in Heav'n
> To dwell, unless by maistring Heav'ns Supreame;
> Nor hope to be my self less miserable
> By what I seek, but others to make such
> As I, though thereby worse to me redound:
> For onely in destroying I finde ease
> To my relentless thoughts; and him destroyd,
> Or won to what may work his utter loss,
> For whom all this was made, all this will soon
> Follow, as to him linkt in weal or woe,
> In wo then; that destruction wide may range.
>
> (IX, 124–134)

Not only has any lingering compassion for the weak disappeared from Satan's character, not only are his physical beauty and brightness dulled, his intellectual power is waning too. For in what follows—and not for public consumption, not for Buncombe, but to himself in soliloquy—he speaks of himself as having "freed from servitude inglorious" nearly half the Angelic host, returning thus to his public utterances of the first two books. Here, too, Satan works himself up in enmity to man, against whom he has no real grievance, and makes a grievance of the very creation of man. He is now so far from his knowledge of God that he attributes to God motives like his own, attributing the creation of man to God's desire to avenge himself upon his enemies. And since man was created to repair the loss from Heaven of himself and his followers, Satan has come to regard man himself as a usurper of the rightful place of the fallen angels.

Satan's envy and rage are further heightened by two considerations, the indignity (again, growing from God's spite) of seeing advanced into the place of angels a creature formed of earth, and the further indignity of seeing angels subjected to the service of the earth-born, flaming Ministers assigned to watch and tend man. This is but another evidence of his disintegration: true angels find it no indignity to attend mankind, to do God's will. Satan does, and, to envy of God and of the true angels, Satan adds envy of man. Frustrated in the attempt to injure God direct, he seeks ill for man, now become the object of his enmity, even at the inevitable cost to himself:

> Revenge, at first though sweet,
> Bitter ere long back on it self recoiles;
> Let it; I reck not, so it light well aim'd,
> Since higher I fall short, on him who next
> Provokes my envie, this new Favorite
> Of Heav'n, this Man of Clay, Son of despite,
> Whom us the more to spite his Maker rais'd
> From dust: spite then with spite is best repaid.
>
> (IX, 171–178)

Surely by thus pointing Satan's enmity to man Milton means to rouse in mankind enmity to Satan.

Hardened as Satan is, determined as these and other lines show him to be, the beauty and innocence of Eve are enough to give him pause when through her willfulness he finds her alone, beyond the reach of Adam's protection:

> her Heav'nly forme
> Angelic, but more soft, and Feminine,
> Her graceful Innocence, her every Aire
> Of gesture or lest action overawd
> His Malice, and with rapine sweet bereav'd
> His fierceness of the fierce intent it brought:
> That space the Evil one abstracted stood
> From his own evil, and for the time remaind
> Stupidly good, of enmitie disarm'd,
> Of guile, of hate, of envie, of revenge;
> But the hot Hell that alwayes in him burnes,
> Though in mid Heav'n, soon ended his delight,
> And tortures him now more, the more he sees
> Of pleasure not for him ordain'd: then soon
> Fierce hate he recollects, and all his thoughts
> Of mischief, gratulating, thus excites.
>
> (IX, 457–472)

"And for the time remaind/ Stupidly good." In that phrase we find still another measure of Satan's evil. Not to do good, but merely to refrain momentarily from evil, and that inadvertently, absently, stupidly, irrationally, is not good at all. Virtue must be more positive, more active a thing than that.

Satan's evil, for which he himself has accepted sole responsibility, is both positive and active, just as his momentary good is not. His evil is as completely evil as the most active good is good. It is deliberate evil. Again and again we have heard him reaffirm the choice made first in Heaven. In Hell we heard him say to Beelzebub,

> of this be sure,
> To do ought good never will be our task,
> But ever to do ill our sole delight,
> As being the contrary to his high will
> Whom we resist.
>
> (I, 158–162)

At the beginning of Book II, when Satan sets the subject for debate, he offers not the choice of war or peace,—"Peace is despaird,/ For who can think Submission?"—but asks

> by what best way,
> Whether of open Warr or covert guile
> We now debate.
>
> (II, 40–42)

In Book IV we saw him deliberately turn his back upon the right that has occurred to him. The frenzied soliloquy at the beginning of Book IX is informed by ill will alone. For all his rage against his lot and against God, his resolution is unchanged, his evil unalloyed. At the moment when he hesitates here in the presence of Eve, his hesitation is not an impulse toward virtue, but merely a moment of abstraction during which the activity of his intellect and of his will is interrupted. From that abstraction he is not long in recollecting himself, in reminding himself that he has come, not from love but from hate; not to exchange Hell for Paradise but to lay waste Paradise; not to taste pleasure but to destroy all pleasure save that only pleasure left for him, the pleasure of destruction. The weakness of Eve does not prevent his self-congratulation that she is alone, that he need not fear the greater intellectual capacity (or the greater physical) of Adam. He proceeds at once to the temptation.

We have seen what epithets Milton chooses to apply to Satan.

We have examined one or two of Satan's public utterances, statements of policy, and the most important of his soliloquies, in
order to understand his motives and his goal. We have heard
him accept—nay boast—the responsibility for the evil that is
to give him divided empire with God. We have found him filled
with Pride, Ambition, and Envy; with Hate, Malice, and Despair; with Wrath, Revengefulness, and Deceit. We have left
only to look briefly at his great action, his attack through Eve
upon the race of men.

The actual temptation is a masterpiece of persuasion. By personal experience Satan has learned well what tempts; by frequent
practice he has become master of lies and sophistries. He begins
with flattery, playing the part, Hanford observes, of a Petrarchan
sonneteer. His purpose is seduction; his address to Eve a "seduction poem," comparable [3] to the speeches of Comus to the Lady
and to the best efforts of the school of courtly love. It begins with
the most skillful flattery, the serpent begging Eve not to wonder
at his boldness nor to disdain his admiration, who alone of all
brute creatures has dared approach her. All living creatures adore
her, but on most her beauty is wasted. Only Adam and himself
have wit to discern it—the celestial beauty of Eve, who should
be seen

> A Goddess among Gods, ador'd and serv'd
> By Angels numberless, thy daily Train.
>   (IX, 547–548)

So early does Satan in glozing words introduce his real purpose,
to arouse in Eve aspirations to Godhead. "Into the Heart of
Eve his words made way." Not, be it noted, into her mind. Eve
is not governed by her reason in this scene, but by her "passions."

Eve's first words are of amazement that a member of brute
creation should speak. She wonders also why the serpent should

---

[3] Cf. *Comus*, ll. 265 ff. The comparison has been noted often.

suddenly become more friendly to her than are the other brutes. Satan is thus carried nearer to his goal in a great stride. Speech, and Reason that accompanies it, he gained because he chanced upon a goodly tree and ate its fruit:

> Sated at length, ere long I might perceave
> Strange alteration in me, to degree
> Of Reason in my inward Powers, and Speech
> Wanted not long, though to this shape retain'd.
>
> (IX, 598–601)

Once given reason, he turned his thoughts "to Speculations high or deep," contemplating all things good, and finding all things good and fair united and surpassed in Eve. Thus his new-found reason led him to come, to gaze and worship. It is Eve's first taste of Godhead. She answers with wit that the serpent's "over-praising leaves in doubt/ The vertue of that Fruit." But she asks to be taken to the tree.

Here Satan's ability to make the worse appear the better reason is given its final test, for Eve remembers the prohibition. It is small wonder that she should be convinced, however, for the argument with which Satan persuades her is so nearly sound as to be reminiscent of *Areopagitica*. It has deceived other critics than Eve and Shelley. In short, the passage is the best of all illustrations of the subtlety of Satan's lies. Asserting the value of knowledge, Satan urges Eve to be

> Deterrd not from atchieving what might leade
> To happier life, knowledge of Good and Evil;
> Of good, how just? of evil, if what is evil
> Be real, why not known, since easier shunnd? [4]
>
> (IX, 696–699)

[4] There is a detailed analysis of Satan's use in this passage of arguments from *Areopagitica* in Irene Samuel's "Platonism in the Poetry of

"What wisdom can there be to choose, what continence to forbear, without the knowledge of evil?" Milton asks in *Areopagitica,* and Satan seems here, like Eve in her argument with Adam,[5] to be uttering a very Miltonic sentiment. Satan's words to Eve's seeming are "impregn'd/ With Reason," and in her musings she echoes his valuation of knowledge:

> What forbids he but to know,
> Forbids us good, forbids us to be wise?
> Such prohibitions binde not.
>   (IX, 758–760)

Thus she is convinced by Satan's lie that sounds like *Areopagitica.* Wherein is it false?

What Satan presents as a means to happier life, the "knowing good by evil," is similarly presented by Milton in *Areopagitica,* but there is an important difference. In *Areopagitica* we find Milton saying

Assuredly we bring not innocence into the world, we bring impurity much rather: that which purifies us is triall, and triall is by what is contrary.[6]

This is the premise upon which the need for knowledge of good by evil is based. In Milton's world as in ours the knowledge of good and evil are inseparable.

It was from out the rinde of one apple tasted, that the knowledge of good and evill as two twins cleaving together leapt forth into the World. And perhaps this is that doom which *Adam* fell into of knowing good and evill, that is to say of knowing good by evill. As there-

---

John Milton," an unpublished dissertation in the library of Cornell University, to be published by the Cornell University Press under the title, *Plato and Milton.* See especially pages 182–187. See also my article, "Eve, the Devil, and *Areopagitica,*" MLQ, V (1944), 429–434, of which the present argument is a redaction. It is reprinted by permission of the publishers.

[5] See Chapter IV, pp. 66–67.   [6] Columbia *Milton,* IV, 311.

fore the state of man now is; what wisdome can there be to choose, what continence to forbeare without the knowledge of evill? [7]

The effect of sin upon mankind is the diminution of the power to distinguish good and evil, a power that must be restored if man is to be restored.[8] The value of knowledge is that it may restore right reason and right conduct. This is a basic Miltonic idea—basic to the plan of Milton's life, to his decision to become a poet (Spenser being a better teacher than Aquinas), to his undertaking of *The Christian Doctrine*. It is expressed in the most explicit terms in *Of Education:*

The end then of Learning is to repair the ruines of our first Parents by regaining to know God aright, and out of that knowledge to love him, to imitate him, to be like him, as we may the neerest by possessing our souls of true vertue, which being united to the heavenly grace of faith makes up the highest perfection.[9]

Before the Fall, the situation of mankind was by no means the same. "This is that doom which *Adam* fell into"; "As therefore the state of man now is"; "Assuredly we bring not innocence into the world." But Adam and Eve, unlike their progeny born in sin, did bring innocence and purity into the world. "From sin and blame entire," they needed no purification; and trial, unnecessary to them, as Adam wisely says will come unsought.

Adam, knowing God, possessed the useful knowledge; we, ignorant since the fall, must seek what Adam lost and must therefore seek it upon new conditions. We have no advantage in the necessity imposed upon us of learning good through evil and Milton does not call it an advantage, but simply a necessity.[10]

As in *Of Education* Milton values knowledge as a means to virtue, "to repair the ruines of our first Parents," so in *Areopagitica* it is not the knowledge itself but the use of it that he values.

---

[7] *Ibid.*, pp. 310–311.   [8] See Chapter V, pp. 113–114.

[9] Columbia *Milton*, IV, 277.

[10] Samuel, "Platonism in the Poetry of John Milton," p. 184. Reprinted by permission of the author.

'This is the part of the argument that Satan suppresses. Since Adam and Eve possess all useful knowledge, he must suppress it. This suppression is the falsehood in his argument. "The knowledge cannot defile . . . if the will and conscience be not defil'd." For Eve and for Adam, however, for whom the awful love of God evidenced by their obedience to his will is the highest duty and the way to highest good (as it is for all mankind), the unsuppressed desire for forbidden knowledge is defilement of will and conscience. Such desire, to leave no spot or blame, may only come (and go) unapproved. The certainty that knowledge sought by will and conscience defiled cannot lead to happier life is the very basis of Satan's attack.

Skillful as it is, this sophistry of Satan's might not of itself be enough. He feigns concern for man and indignation at the wrong done him, arguing from his own pretended experience. Is there death in the tree? He has touched and tasted, and is a living example of its virtue. He now not only lives, but lives at a higher level of existence than fate (not God, let it be noted) intended for him. Can that be ill for man that is open to the beasts? Such trespass, surely, is too petty to arouse the wrath of a just God, who must rather praise the courage that would brave death for a better life. A just God must. "Not just, not God," and neither to be obeyed nor to be feared.

What can God's motive be? Obviously, Satan says, to keep men

> low and ignorant,
> His worshippers; he knows that in the day
> Ye Eate thereof, your Eyes that seem so cleere,
> Yet are but dim, shall perfetly be then
> Opn'd and cleerd, and ye shall be as Gods.
>
> (IX, 704–708)

Is this what death means, "by putting off Human, to put on Gods?"

Goddess Humane, reach then, and freely taste.
He ended, and his words replete with guile
Into her heart too easie entrance won.

(IX, 732–734)

The whole argument, of course, is built upon a false example, upon the original deception that it is the serpent who speaks and upon the lie that he himself has eaten of the fruit. In the guise of an angel, as in the dream, Satan might have failed. But here he is visibly a snake, audibly speaking, endowed with reason, of brute made human—by virtue of the tree, he says. And Eve is hungry. The combination of her hunger, his flattery, the aspirations to godhead and to forbidden knowledge that he has aroused in her, and above all his example, is too much. Eve argues further with herself but briefly, and the moment toward which Satan in the action and Milton in the poem have been building has come. Eve eats. "Back to the Thicket slunk/ The guiltie Serpent."

This then, this loss of good to all mankind, this seduction of innocent Eve, this is the end to which Satan's energy and magnificence are devoted. This, to return to Shelley's words, is the purpose Satan has conceived to be excellent. This, at any rate, he has achieved. His part as active agent in *Paradise Lost* has ended. He has been seen author of evil, enemy to God and Man, to be abhorred by the good and condemned by the intelligent. Those who do not find him abhorrent have misread the poem. They will do well to ask whether their liking for Satan does not spring from enmity to God.

CHAPTER IV

Man's Guilt

ADAM AND EVE are capable of obedience to God, but like the later Satanists, Eve prefers to believe the devil. Adam places his love of Eve above his love of God. Of their free will they are disobedient.

The part of Adam and Eve in the action of *Paradise Lost* is less spectacular than that of Satan. They are the stake for which Satan plays, and as such are passive rather than active, the recipients of action rather than the initiators of it. Although they are agents in the central incident and although all the action of which they are not chief agents converges on them, the central incident of *Paradise Lost,* after all, is but the eating of an apple. Milton tells us at the beginning of the ninth book, the book in which the incident occurs, that this is an event and a subject

> Not less but more Heroic than the wrauth
> Of stern *Achilles* on his Foe pursu'd
> Thrice Fugitive about *Troy* Wall.
>
> (IX, 14–16)

It is indeed for Milton and his time, as Tillyard points out, and should be for us, the greatest subject in the world, overwhelming in its implications and in its consequences. Even though it is an event which shook the whole physical universe, however, and which determined the fate of all mankind, the incident is in itself trivial. If more heroic than the wrath of Achilles, it is less spectacular—and less spectacular than the war in Heaven, than the rage of Satan, or the wrath of God.

Nevertheless it is Adam and Eve who are important. They are

the central characters in the poem: their conduct raises some of the most important points in the argument. Their characters and their actions therefore require close examination. Why do they deserve, with Satan and his followers, the punishment to which they are condemned? What extenuating circumstance accounts for the different treatment given to them and to the fallen angels? What, exactly, is their sin? To answer these questions will be a large part of the task of the present and the succeeding chapters. We shall have to examine the conduct of Adam and Eve separately, for they are not equal and they are not alike. Both representative of the race, Adam is also man and Eve woman. But Tillyard points to a confusion that runs through the ninth book, if not through all the parts of the poem concerned with Paradise:

> . . . it is not always clear for what Adam and Eve stand. Do they stand for humanity or for man and woman? When Eve in evil hour stretches forth her rash hand for the fruit, does Milton intend her rashness to be universally human or specifically feminine?[1]

Tillyard's answer to his own question is that Milton mixes the two meanings, but that in the end his old grudge against women gets the better of his conscious intentions. This seems to imply that, for Tillyard, Milton's conscious intention is to let Eve stand for humanity, not specifically for womankind, but that his memory of Mary Powell diverts him. If *Paradise Lost* were allegorical as the *Faerie Queene* is, it would be easier to be sure. But even when, as here, we regard it as an argument, we must realize that it is a story first. Sin and Death are allegorical figures, realized abstractions. Adam and Eve (and Satan) are not abstractions. They are real agents, individual agents, who also happen to stand for the race. Eve before the fall is innocent womanhood, no doubt, and after the fall is guilty womanhood. She is also mankind. She is not innocence and guilt.

[1] *Milton* (London, Chatto and Windus; New York, Dial Press, 1930), pp. 257–258. Reprinted by permission of the publishers.

Whether or not Adam represents his sex, specifically, and Eve hers, both represent humanity. God, their creator, whom they know to be infinitely good, infinitely wise, and infinitely powerful, prohibits the eating of the apple. Adam and Eve choose to eat. In the fantastic perversity which prefers an apple to God, they are not masculine or feminine, but human. In the particular weaknesses that lead them to this choice, Eve may stand for woman and Adam for man, but in the crucial point, their lack of faith and the disobedience that springs from it, they represent humanity. The obligation to obey is stressed again and again in the account of Eden.

Appropriately, Hanford observes, after the description of the beauties of Eden, the first words we hear from Adam are of gratitude to God. To the twentieth-century reader, watchful for the unconscious and suspicious of professed meanings, Adam's gratitude may seem somewhat imperfect, since by easy transition from gratitude for God's manifold gifts Adam turns to the single prohibition. It may seem to some of us, and to Satan, that the prohibition was unreasonable and that Adam is therefore irked by it. To Milton the prohibition was not unreasonable, nor did it seem unreasonable to Adam, who speaks:

> needs must the power
> That made us, and for us this ample World
> Be infinitly good, and of his good
> As liberal and free as infinite,
> That rais'd us from the dust and plac't us here
> In all this happiness, who at his hand
> Have nothing merited, nor can performe
> Aught whereof hee hath need, hee who requires
> From us no other service then to keep
> This one, this easie charge, of all the Trees
> In Paradise that bear delicious fruit

> So various, not to taste that onely Tree
> Of knowledge.
>
> (IV, 412–424)

Adam's gratitude and his remembrance of the prohibition are indeed in close juxtaposition here, but not necessarily to indicate a lurking discontent. There is the narrative function of the speech to consider. Satan, listening, must be told of the prohibition so that he may engineer the fall. It is for his ears, for the sake of narrative economy, that mention of the prohibition is so quickly brought into the dialogue. Satan's response is to exclaim,

> O fair foundation laid whereon to build
> Thir ruine!
>
> (IV, 521–522)

It is for this that Adam comes so quickly to the subject, not from rebelliousness. Of rebelliousness there is no hint at all—except in the juxtaposition of ideas. Perhaps lest we think we find rebelliousness, Milton has Adam go on at once to reaffirm his acceptance of the prohibition, calling it

> This one, this easie charge, ...
> The only sign of our obedience left
> Among so many signes of power and rule
> Conferrd upon us, and Dominion giv'n
> Over all other Creatures that possess
> Earth, Aire, and Sea. Then let us not think hard
> One easie prohibition, who enjoy
> Free leave so large to all things else.
>
> (IV, 421–434)

Eve has a double obligation of obedience—an obligation to obey Adam as well as God. In writing of Eden, Milton is concerned not only with man's duty to God, but also with man's duty to man—with human relationships and human conduct.

Given the human beings he has to work with, two only, it is the relationship between man and woman, husband and wife, that he may treat. It is a subject upon which Milton has thought much and upon which he has written earlier—upon which he thought before as well as after his first marriage.

If the world since Milton's time has seen something of the practice and has accepted the theory of emancipated woman, Milton had not. He shows us Adam and Eve first through the eyes of Satan, who

> Saw undelighted all delight, all kind
> Of living Creatures new to sight and strange:
> Two of far nobler shape erect and tall,
> Godlike erect, with native Honour clad
> In naked Majestie seemd Lords of all
> And worthie seemd, for in thir looks Divine
> The image of thir glorious Maker shon,
> Truth, wisdome, Sanctitude severe and pure,
> Severe but in true filial freedom plac't;
> Whence true autoritie in men; . . . .
>
> (IV, 286–295)

But as they seem not equal, neither are they:

> For contemplation hee and valour formd,
> For softness shee and sweet attractive Grace,
> Hee for God only, shee for God in him:
> His fair large Front and Eye sublime declar'd
> Absolute rule.
>
> (IV, 297–301)

Absolute rule this means and Milton meant it to mean. He is saying that Adam, the husband, is the head, the fount of reason in family life, and should rule—should be granted obedience, that is to say, not exacting it by force. Eve's subjection is "re-

quired with gentle sway,/ And by her yeilded, by him best receiv'd." It is because Eve, with specious arguments, fails in submission that she is exposed alone to the blandishments of Satan.
It is because Adam fails in his attempt to rule with "gentle
sway" that with some semblance of obedience she is so exposed.
Even before the fall, Eve is the weaker vessel, and in this she is
representative of womankind. Her relative weakness is in the
very form of woman. As the uprightness of both Adam and Eve
is godlike, one mark of their dignity, so the brow of Adam marks
him for contemplation and valor, for thought and for action,
and his eye for rule. As Eve is formed for softness, so her vinelike
wanton ringlets mark her for subjection.

Eve accepts the obligation. As the first words we hear uttered
by Adam are of gratitude and submission to God, Eve's are of
submission to Adam and gratitude to God:

> O thou for whom
> And from whom I was formd flesh of thy flesh,
> And without whom am to no end, my Guide
> And Head, what thou hast said is just and right.
> For wee to him indeed all praises owe.
>
> (IV, 440–444)

And then in loving memory Eve returns to the day of her creation, dwelling at some length upon the incident of her reflection
in a pool—an incident, Hanford says, that serves to point out the
weakness that is to entrap her. We have seen that in the temptation Eve's vanity does twofold service to Satan, once securing
her attention to his discourse, and again (translated into the
hybris of seeking Godhead) as an important motive in her fall.
Here, however, she ends her memory of her first meeting with
Adam and of her first preference of her own image to his sterner
apparition, by observing that she has from that time come to see

> How beauty is excelld by manly grace
> And wisdom, which alone is truly fair.
>   (IV, 490–491)

The scene is a love scene, a pastoral idyl, showing our first parents in complete and peaceful happiness, the happiness of virtue, and marked as an example to men by Milton's "digression" on the purity of wedded love. After an interlude recounting Uriel's warning to Gabriel of Satan's presence, it is resumed as such. Evening has come, and Adam bids to rest.

> To whom thus *Eve* with perfet beauty adornd.
> My Author and Disposer, what thou bidst
> Unargu'd I obey; so God ordains,
> God is thy Law, thou mine: to know no more
> Is womans happiest knowledge and her praise.
>   (IV, 634–638)

The same speech gives her further opportunity to assert her love, her happiness, her joy in the world, all dependent upon her love for Adam. Alas, that in the crucial moment she refrains neither from argument nor from disobedience!

When Book V opens, Eve has had her dream, and has been saved by the continuing presence of the guardian angels, who interrupted Satan. She tells her dream to Adam, who excuses and explains it in terms that bear directly upon the understanding of Milton's ethic:

> know that in the Soule
> Are many lesser Faculties that serve
> Reason as chief.
>   (V, 100–102)

The Fancy, combining the material of the senses into various combinations, is under constant censorship of reason. But in dreams, reason asleep, a "mimic Fansie" wakes, "misjoyning shapes," combining remembered words and deeds into false combinations. In such circumstances,

> Evil into the mind of God or Man
> May come and go, so unapprov'd, and leave
> No spot or blame behind.

(V, 117–119)

As long as evil thoughts pass, then, unapproved by reason, and not translated into action, they carry no blame with them. It is another affirmation of reason as the means of determining proper action, with the clear implication so often repeated in Milton that all wrong is contrary to reason. Nevertheless, the dream is the beginning of the temptation, the beginning of the fall, and serves notice on the reader of Eve's readiness for temptation. The desires that are to lead to her downfall have been aroused in her; her liability to them is clear; and the dream is in the background of her experience when she later insists upon the separation from Adam in order, we shall see, to subject herself to temptation.[2]

---

[2] Dr. Irene Samuel has called my attention to an illuminating parallel (I think hitherto unnoted) at the beginning of the ninth book of Plato's *Republic* (in *The Dialogues of Plato*, tr. B. Jowett, New York and London, 1892, Vol. III, pp. 280–281).

Certain of the unnecessary pleasures and appetites I conceive to be unlawful; every one appears to have them, but in some persons they are controlled by the laws and by reason, and the better desires prevail over them—either they are wholly banished or they become few and weak; while in the case of others they are stronger, and there are more of them.

Which appetites do you mean?

I mean those which are awake when the reasoning and human and ruling power is asleep; then the wild beast within us, gorged with meat or drink, starts up and having shaken off sleep, goes forth to satisfy his desires; and there is no conceivable folly or crime—not excepting incest or any other unnatural union, or parricide, or the eating of forbidden food—which at such a time, when he has parted

The coming of Raphael after the dream—or rather his departure later—marks the end of a phase of existence for Adam and Eve. Heretofore they have been under the direct protection of emissaries from Heaven, of whom Raphael is the last. From him there is much for Adam to learn, and his visit, to which four books of *Paradise Lost* are devoted, is of great importance to the narrative as to the argument. Through him Adam learns, and we listening, of the revolt of Satan and its cause in Satan's pride and envy at the elevation of the Son, of the war in Heaven, its result, and the consequent enmity of Satan toward men, with much more of the constitution of angels and of the creation of the world. Finally Adam gives an account of his life since his own creation, of the creation of Eve and of his love for her.

At the very beginning of his visit, the angel's first words (after greeting and refreshment) are a warning:

---

company with all shame and sense, a man may not be ready to commit.

Most true, he said.

But when a man's pulse is healthy and temperate, and when before going to sleep he has awakened his rational powers, and fed them on noble thoughts and enquiries, collecting himself in meditation; after having first indulged his appetites neither too much nor too little, but just enough to lay them to sleep, and prevent them and their enjoyments and pains from interfering with the higher principle—which he leaves in the solitude of pure abstraction, free to contemplate and aspire to the knowledge of the unknown, whether in the past, present, or future: when again he has allayed the passionate element, if he has a quarrel against any one—I say, when after pacifying the two irrational principles, he rouses up the third, which is reason, before he takes his rest, then, as you know, he attains truth most nearly, and is least likely to be the sport of fantastic and lawless visions.

I quite agree.

In saying this I have been running into a digression; but the point which I desire to note is that in all of us, even in good men, there is a lawless wild-beast nature, which peers out in sleep.

> O *Adam,* one Almightie is, from whom
> All things proceed, and up to him return,
> If not deprav'd from good,
>
> (V, 469–472)

and the speech ends with a repetition of the warning in more specific terms:

> If ye be found obedient, and retain
> Unalterably firm his love entire
> Whose progenie you are. Mean while enjoy
> Your fill what happiness this happie state
> Can comprehend, incapable of more.
>
> (V, 501–505)

Adam is startled by the conditional clause, by the suggested possibility that he and Eve may be found wanting, so unquestioned to him is proper gratitude to God and love for Him

> But say,
> What meant that caution joind, *if ye be found*
> *Obedient?* can we want obedience then
> To him, or possibly his love desert
> Who formd us from the dust, and plac'd us here
> Full to the utmost measure of what bliss
> Human desires can seek or apprehend?
>
> (V, 512–518)

To the reader, knowing the event, Adam's confidence is tragic irony. From Raphael it elicits further warning, a reaffirmation of the crucial point of man's freedom, so often urged throughout the whole poem:

> That thou art happie, owe to God;
> That thou continu'st such, owe to thy self,
> That is, to thy obedience; therein stand.
> This was that caution giv'n thee; be advis'd.
> God made thee perfet, not immutable;

> And good he made thee, but to persevere
> He left it in thy power, ordaind thy will
> By nature free, not over-rul'd by Fate
> Inextricable, or strict necessity;
> Our voluntarie service he requires,
> Not our necessitated.
> (V, 520–530)

And then he comes, in a few lines, to the awful warning example of Satan:

> My self and all th'Angelic Host that stand
> In sight of God enthron'd, our happie state
> Hold, as you yours, while our obedience holds;
> On other surety none; freely we serve,
> Because wee freely love, as in our will
> To love or not; in this we stand or fall:
> And som are fall'n, to disobedience fall'n,
> And so from Heav'n to deepest Hell; O fall
> From what high state of bliss into what woe!
> (V, 535–543)

Adam reaffirms his acceptance of the sole command. He knows himself in "will and deed created free." In spite of the capacity for disobedience that this implies he has been and remains confident

> that we never shall forget to love
> Our maker, and obey him whose command .
> Single, is yet so just.
> (V, 550–552)

Nevertheless, what Raphael says of fallen angels moves him to some doubt and to more desire to hear. Raphael, with the qualification that it is not easy to translate heavenly events into terms of human understanding, agrees to try. From the story as it is

told, Adam is to learn what it is needful to him to know—not only
by the unhappy example of Satan and the punishment meted out
to him, but in the fifth and sixth books by the converse example
of Abdiel, the faithful, and the reward of praise and glory given
him. What Adam learns, the reader learns.

The warnings to Adam are made very specific. At the end of
Book VI, when the account of the war in Heaven is concluded,
comes a paragraph of great importance:

> Thus measuring things in Heav'n by things on Earth
> At thy request, and that thou maist beware
> By what is past, to thee I have reveal'd
> What might have else to human Race bin hid;
> The discord which befel, and Warr in Heav'n
> Among th'Angelic Powers, and the deep fall
> Of those too high aspiring, who rebelld
> With *Satan,* hee who envies now thy state,
> Who now is plotting how he may seduce
> Thee also from obedience, that with him
> Bereavd of happiness thou maist partake
> His punishment, Eternal miserie;
> Which would be all his solace and revenge,
> As a despite don against the most High,
> Thee once to gaine Companion of his woe.
> But list'n not to his Temptations, warne
> Thy weaker; let it profit thee to have heard
> By terrible Example the reward
> Of disobedience; firm they might have stood,
> Yet fell; remember, and fear to transgress.
>
> (VI, 893–912)

Here the purpose of Raphael's narrative (and of Milton's too)
is affirmed: "that thou maist beware/ By what is past." The fall
of the angels is explained: they were "too high aspiring." The

motive for Satan's enmity to man is stated: envy and the hope
that in the fall of man spite may be done to God. The painful
consequences of sin are pointed out, "By terrible Example." The
freedom of choice, the responsibility of the agent to remain true
is emphasized again: "Firm they might have stood,/ Yet fell."
Finally the application of the whole narrative is brought home to
Adam by the imperative addressed specifically to him: "remember, and fear to transgress." Henceforth if Adam falls, his fall is
inexcusable. He knows his enemy, the motives of his enemy, and
he knows his duty.

In another passage which the event makes ironic, Adam accepts
the warning for what it is, addressing Raphael as one

> by favour sent
> Down from the Empyrean to forewarne
> Us timely of what might else have bin our loss,
> Unknown, which human knowledg could not reach:
> For which to the infinitly Good we owe
> Immortal thanks, and his admonishment
> Receave with solemne purpose to observe
> Immutably his sovran will, the end
> Of what we are.

> (VII, 72–80)

But there is still more for Adam to learn about the world in which
he lives and about its creation. He is to learn that he himself has
been created to provide a race that will repair the loss to Heaven
of the fallen angels. Finally he must learn about himself. His
desire for knowledge temperately satisfied, Adam tells Raphael
what he himself remembers since his own creation. What Adam
has to say of the creation of Eve, of his need for her before her
creation, and of his love for her, leads Raphael to utter another
warning, very specific indeed. Since the whole passage very
strongly foreshadows the fall, we must quote again at length.

Adam speaking of his delight in Eve contrasts it with his delight in the world about him,

> delight indeed, but such
> As us'd or not, works in the mind no change,
> Nor vehement desire.
>
> (VIII, 524–526)

Not so his joy in Eve:

> here
> Farr otherwise, transported I behold,
> Transported touch; here passion first I felt,
> Commotion strange, in all enjoyments else
> Superior and unmov'd, here onely weake
> Against the charm of Beauties powerful glance.
>
> (VIII, 528–533)

He seeks some excuse for the weakness he finds in himself, attributing it to some flaw in his composition, or to a change in his composition resultant from the creation of Eve:

> Or Nature faild in mee, and left some part
> Not proof enough such Object to sustain,
> Or from my side subducting, took perhaps
> More then enough.
>
> (VIII, 534–537)

Or, if it is not some deficiency in himself for which he is not responsible, then perhaps Eve has been made too beautiful for male resistance. That he is too much subject to her charms, whether from weakness in himself or excess of them, remains quite clear, just as it remains clear that he is really the superior:

> For well I understand in the prime end
> Of Nature her th'inferiour, in the mind
> And inward Faculties, which most excell.
>
> (VIII, 540–542)

Even so, her (after all only slightly) inferior qualities in conjunction with her beauty seem superior:

> yet when I approach
> Her loveliness, so absolute she seems
> And in herself compleat, so well to know
> Her own, that what she wills to do or say,
> Seems wisest, vertuousest, discreetest, best;
> All higher knowledge in her presence falls
> Degraded, Wisdom in discourse with her
> Looses discount'nanc't, and like folly shewes;
> Authority and Reason on her waite,
> As one intended first, not after made
> Occasionally; and to consummate all,
> Greatness of mind and nobleness thir seat
> Build in her loveliest, and create an awe
> About her, as a guard Angelic plac't.
>
> (VIII, 546–559)

This anticipatory attempt at self-exculpation is immediately rejected. The angel will have none of it:

> Accuse not Nature, she hath don her part;
> Do thou but thine.
>
> (VIII, 561–562)

Adam's departure from the demands of his intelligence in submitting his judgment to Eve's is also discussed:

> and be not diffident
> Of Wisdom, she deserts thee not, if thou
> Dismiss not her, when most thou needst her nigh,
> By attributing overmuch to things
> Less excellent, as thou thy self perceav'st.
> For what admir'st thou, what transports thee so,
> An outside? fair no doubt, and worthy well

> Thy cherishing, thy honouring, and thy love,
> Not thy subjection: weigh with her thy self;
> Then value.

(VIII, 562–571)

Adam, for contemplation and for valor formed, is rightly the head; Eve, for softness, must be subject. In the family as in Heaven the fittest to rule must rule. Above all, Adam is warned not to let the physical relationship overwhelm him; it is shared by beasts, and would not be so

>   if aught
> Therein enjoy'd were worthy to subdue
> The Soule of Man, or passion in him move.

(VIII, 583–585)

Instead, he is admonished,

> What higher in her societie thou findst
> Attractive, human, rational, love still;
> In loving thou dost well, in passion not,
> Wherein true Love consists not; love refines
> The thoughts, and heart enlarges, hath his seat
> In Reason, and is judicious, is the scale
> By which to heav'nly Love thou maist ascend.

(VIII, 586–592)

Adam, half-abashed, in reply minimizes the extent of his subjection, protesting that it is after all neither Eve's "outside" nor physical love that delights him so much as the graceful acts and "thousand decencies that daily flow/ From all her words and actions," acts that declare theirs a genuine union of mind. What he has disclosed, he protests, is but his inward impulse, an impulse not approved by his intelligence. The evil is still unapproved. He is therefore still free from bondage to sense and passion.

As the dream foreshadows the Fall of Eve, this dialogue fore-

warns the reader of Adam's readiness for temptation and of the
probable source of it. Raphael is forewarned as well and remains
dissatisfied, ending his parting disquisition on the love of angels
with a last admonishment:

> Be strong, live happie, and love, but first of all
> Him whom to love is to obey, and keep
> His great command; take heed least Passion sway
> Thy Judgement to do aught, which else free Will
> Would not admit; thine and of all thy Sons
> The weal or woe in thee is plac't; beware.
> I in thy persevering shall rejoyce,
> And all the Blest: stand fast; to stand or fall
> Free in thine own Arbitrement it lies.
> Perfet within, no outward aid require;
> And all temptation to transgress repel.
>
> (VIII, 633–643)

Here is reaffirmed the first obligation, to love God and to obey
his one command. Here is again specific warning that danger lies
in passion, and that to be governed by passion is to lose freedom.
Here is a reminder to Adam of the consequences of failure to
himself and to his posterity. Here, finally, is still another affirmation that Adam is free to stand or fall, no outward aid requiring.

After the visit of Raphael, Adam knows all he needs to know.
He knows the enmity of Satan and the weakness of himself, the
outward and the inward danger. Now without aid he may stand.
Now without aid he must stand—or fall. The departure of
Raphael is the end of special protection. Adam is on his own,
and the establishment of his full responsibility is marked by the
prologue to Book IX:

> No more of talk where God or Angel Guest
> With Man, as with his Friend, familiar us'd
> To sit indulgent, and with him partake

Rural repast, permitting him the while
Venial discourse unblam'd; I now must change
Those Notes to Tragic.

(IX, 1–6)

Without Satan, Adam and Eve would not have been exposed
to temptation, unless, conceivably, like Satan they were exposed
to it from within. Of that possibility there is no hint. Satan therefore shares the responsibility for Man's fall. But he only shares
it. Adam and Eve are sufficient to stand firm against any temptation Satan can put in their way, and should stand firm. The responsibility is theirs as well as his. Their fall is their own, and
we can trace its stages. We have taken it to begin, in a sense, with
the first temptation: Eve's dream. It continues, progressing, when
Eve forgets her proper submission and chooses to separate herself
from Adam.

In the argument with Adam that results in the separation,
Eve, like Satan at the tree, employs arguments from *Areopagitica*
—arguments which do not apply to the objections which Adam
raises and which do not apply to the situation.[3] Adam is convinced by them no more than he is convinced by her argument
that two shifts of plant-pruners are necessary. As later he eats
of the apple himself, against his better judgment, so here he gives
grudging consent against his better judgment. His complaisance
is correlative to Eve's willfullness. Overcome here, perhaps, as
later, by "femal charm," he ignores his duty, ignores Raphael's
admonition that he weigh himself with Eve, ignores his own
superiority and what is proper to it.

Eve, wrong in the argument, is wrong in her stubbornness, in
her pique, and in her conduct. Nor is her conduct based upon the
reasons which she first urges. Eve's opportunity in the colloquy

[3] For a detailed discussion of this passage, see "Eve, the Devil, and
Areopagitica," *MLQ*, V (1944), 429–434.

with Adam is to demonstrate her obedience. Instead, she fails in
obedience and goes forth not in order to prune more roses and
waste less time, but actually to seek temptation. Her arguments
are but the rationalization of her desire—the desire for temptation which, following the dream, is another step toward her
ultimate fall.

Although she seeks temptation, however, Eve does not intend
to yield to it. She does succumb, Tillyard says, because of her
triviality of mind:

Nor is there any need of a great wave of passion to overwhelm her
resolution. Eve shows little strength of feeling: it is not so much excess of passion as triviality of mind that is her ruin. She is a prey to a
variety of feelings, but it is always this triviality that allows her thus
to be preyed on. First comes susceptibility to flattery. . . . Then she
is unwary. . . . Just before following Satan to the Tree she is called
'our credulous Mother.' Confronted by the Tree for a moment she
recollects herself and makes a faint resistance; but a single long speech
of Satan is enough to overcome it. . . . And when he ceases speaking,
Milton writes (733-734):

> He ended, and his words replete with guile
> Into her heart too easie entrance won.[4]

Eve is vain, and the susceptibility to flattery that results from
her vanity is useful to Satan. She is unwary, not looking for Satan
in the serpent. She is credulous, for she believes a liar. Her resistance is insufficient, for Satan's words find "too easie entrance"
into her heart. But the flattery that catches her attention in
Satan's "glozing proem" is extremely skillful, as we have seen.
Appealing to her vanity, it leads her to the *hybris* of aspiring to
Godhead. It is that, not the flattery, which is the temptation.
Eve is unwary; but the devil is disguised and she is overwhelmed
by curiosity and amazement to hear a serpent speak. She is credulous; but she is confronted by the very father of lies, and hypocrisy

---

[4] *Milton* (London, Chatto and Windus; New York, Dial Press, 1930),
p. 260. Reprinted by permission of the publishers.

is the "only evil that walks/ Invisible except to God alone," recognized by neither man nor angel. Even Uriel we have seen deceived by Satan. Eve yields too easily, but any surrender to temptation is too easy, and inexcusable. Sufficient to have withstood temptation she should have done so. But to be deceived by the deceiver of angels is hardly proof of "trivial" mentality.

The temptation itself is very great—to be

> A Goddess among Gods, ador'd and serv'd
> By Angels numberless,
>
> (IX, 547–548)

and to have godlike knowledge. So Satan plans it:

> Hence I will excite thir minds
> With more desire to know, and to reject
> Envious commands, invented with designe
> To keep them low whom knowledge might exalt
> Equal with Gods; aspiring to be such,
> They taste and die.
>
> (IV, 522–527)

It is the temptation before which Satan himself fell, urged with arguments of great force:

To overcome her hesitation Satan musters all his eloquence. . . . He employs all the arguments which scepticism can suggest against an arbitrary and irrational command, and, with the cooperating aid of mere physical appetite at the noontide hour, prevails. Eve unconsciously falls into his own train of reasoning.[5]

We have seen how eloquent Satan is. Moreover Eve has prepared herself to be persuaded by anticipating some of Satan's arguments. Some critics have also been persuaded by these arguments and dismiss the whole justification because God's command was ar-

[5] Hanford, *A Milton Handbook*, (3d ed., New York, F. S. Crofts and Co., 1939), p. 212. These passages are reprinted by permission of the publishers.

bitrary and irrational, concluding therefore that Eve was not wrong to eat. To be convinced by such eloquence from such a source and in the presence of such temptations, we repeat, need not indicate triviality of mind. It may indicate defilement of will and conscience.

Nevertheless, Eve's is a fault of mind; her fall, like all sin, is a departure from reason, her case different from Adam's in that she is deceived where his "higher intellectual" is not. Perhaps we quarrel only with the word triviality.

"Eve is deluded in her weakness," Hanford says,

but once confronted by the tree of prohibition she recognizes clearly the guilt involved. This is Milton's modification or interpretation of the Biblical statement "the woman was deceived." He could not have her sin unconsciously.[6]

No more he could. Intention is everything, and Eve's intention must be to disobey. Satan may employ deception as much as he likes in an argument designed to persuade Eve to eat of the forbidden fruit, but she must recognize the fruit for what it is. She may be misled into false reasoning by his lies, but unless her disobedience is deliberate, it is none. The one point on which she may not be deceived is the identity of the tree. In the debate with Eve before the separation, Adam points out specifically that man's real danger lies within himself: "Against his will he can receave no harme."

Adam in his warning to Eve makes it clear both to Eve and to the reader that the obligation of right conduct does indeed include the obligation of right thought, that right conduct is based upon right thinking, for he again explains freedom in terms of reason and emphasizes the need for constant intellectual alertness:

> But God left free the Will, for what obeyes
> Reason, is free, and Reason he made right,

[6] *Ibid.*, pp. 211-212.

> But bid her well beware, and still erect,
> Least by some faire appeering good surpris'd
> She dictate false, and misinforme the Will
> To do what God expressly hath forbid.
>
>   (IX, 351–356)

No warning could anticipate a danger in more specific terms. For Eve, too, therefore, all justice has been fulfilled. She too has been rendered inexcusable, and Adam's speech is another of the many ironic anticipations in the poem and another commentary on the action. It tells us in exact terms what happens to Eve. Eve here told to beware becomes unwary Eve. Specifically warned against specious reasoning, she follows Satan's falsehoods until she falls into his train of thought; her reason misinforms her will "To do what God expressly hath forbid." Failure to obey the "arbitrary and irrational tabu" of which Grierson speaks is a failure in reason.

Even though we insist that neither her resistance nor her intellect need be called trivial, Eve is after all intellectually inferior to Adam. Therefore Satan hoped to find her alone. In this, as in her susceptibility to flattery, Eve is meant to typify womankind. In the effective point of the temptation, the aspiration to Godhead, she stands for the race.

That this aspiration is the central motive leading to the fall, Merritt Hughes has a persuasive argument, in which he quotes from the *Reason of Church Government* to the effect that

Lucifer, before Adam, was the first prelate angel; and both he, as is commonly thought, and our forefather Adam, as we all know, for aspiring above their orders, were miserably degraded.[7]

When Satan approaches Eve in the dream, Hughes points out, it is to persuade her that the fruit of the tree is the means to Godhead, and God himself, predicting the fall, says

---

[7] Merritt Y. Hughes, ed., *Paradise Lost* (Garden City, N.Y., 1935), Introduction, pp. xxxii ff.

> Man disobeying,
> Disloyal breaks his fealtie, and sinns
> Against the high Supremacie of Heav'n,
> Affecting God-head, and so loosing all.
>   (III, 203–206)

In the actual temptation this is true for Eve. She, representing the race we therefore think, accepts the serpent's assurance that it is envy on the part of the gods that accounts for the prohibition. In her very act of eating, Milton reminds us, this motive is present:

> Intent now wholly on her taste, naught else
> Regarded, such delight till then, as seemd,
> In Fruit she never tasted, whether true
> Or fansied so, through expectation high
> Of knowledg, nor was God-head from her thought.
>   (IX, 786–790)

The temptation and fall are not simple, of course. There are other elements than *hybris*. Eve seeks knowledge as a means to godhead, but she does seek knowledge. Vanity is part of her weakness. Hunger is part. "In making Eve fall through vanity and curiosity for new experience," says Hanford,

Adam through blind passion, Milton points to what he believes the characteristic weaknesses respectively of man and woman.[8]

But the sin of *hybris* is not characteristically feminine and neither is hunger. Appetite and pride are human frailties.

Adam falls through passion, says Hanford in this passage. Through gregariousness, says Tillyard:

It is certainly not sensuality. Adam's passions are in no wise roused: he merely voices the natural human instinct of comradeship with his kind.[9]

---

[8] *A Milton Handbook*, p. 213.

[9] *Milton*, (London, Chatto and Windus; New York, Dial Press, 1930), p. 262. Reprinted by permission of the publishers.

Again we find ourselves in disagreement, although perhaps again only with Tillyard's words. In the sense in which he is using the word, Adam's passions are at the moment not aroused. The appeal is not to the senses. But neither is it Adam's despair at the thought of a lonely existence that determines him.

> with thee
> Certain my resolution is to Die;
> How can I live without thee, how forgoe
> They sweet Converse and Love so dearly joyn'd,
> To live again in these wilde Woods forlorn?
> Should God create another *Eve,* and I
> Another Rib afford, yet loss of thee
> Would never from my heart; no no, I feel
> The Link of Nature draw me; Flesh of Flesh,
> Bone of my Bone thou art, and from thy State
> Mine never shall be parted, bliss or woe.
> (IX, 906–916)

And again,

> However I with thee have fixt my Lot,
> Certain to undergoe like doom, if Death
> Consort with thee, Death is to mee as Life;
> So forcible within my heart I feel
> The Bond of Nature draw me to my owne,
> My own in thee, for what thou art is mine;
> Our State cannot be severd, we are one,
> One Flesh; to loose thee were to loose my self.
> (IX, 952–959)

The second affirmation comes at the end of the passage in which Adam, rationalizing, with the decision made, tries to convince himself that there is still a possibility of escaping the consequences

of sin. It is a return to the real reason on the basis of which his
decision was immediate.

It is not, then, the loss of companionship that Adam cannot
accept: it is the loss of Eve. Raphael has earlier rejected Adam's
plea of the link of nature. We have heard him warn Adam to

> take heed lest Passion sway
> Thy Judgement to do aught, which else free Will
> Would not admit;
>
> (VIII, 635–637)

telling him also to love,

> but first of all
> Him whom to love is to obey, and keep
> His great command.
>
> (VIII, 633–635)

And here is Adam's sin. Unlike Christian in *Pilgrim's Progress*
he puts his love of Eve before his love of God. His decision made,

> she embrac'd him, and for joy
> Tenderly wept, much won that he his Love
> Had so enobl'd, as of choice to incurr
> Divine displeasure for her sake, or Death.
> In recompence (for such compliance bad
> Such recompence best merits) from the bough
> She gave him of that fair enticing Fruit
> With liberal hand: he scrupl'd not to eat
> Against his better knowledge, not deceav'd,
> But fondly overcome with Femal charm.
>
> (IX, 990–999)

Tillyard points out an inconsistency here, since "Adam had made
up his mind before Eve exercised her charms on him: her caresses
were superfluous." They are superfluous, no doubt, as Eve's noon-

tide hunger was superfluous to her temptation. But like her hunger, they add to the complex of the temptation the physical impulse. As she was overcome by desire for forbidden knowledge and by her aspiration to Godhead, plus hunger, so Adam is overcome by uxoriousness, by his love for Eve plus his physical desire for her. If at the moment her embraces are but a minor factor in the temptation, it is still "Femal charm," her "sweet Converse and love so dearly joyn'd" that leads him to compliance bad and to submit his own superior to Eve's inferior judgment. This, we may agree with Hanford, is for Milton the typical weakness of the male animal.

Sensuality, then, for both, is but a minor temptation, contributing to the major. Like the aspirations of Satan and Eve, like Satan's pride and envy and hate, like Adam's uxoriousness, and like all the other remissnesses involved in the fall itself as listed in the *Christian Doctrine*,[10] it is a departure from reason and hence a sin. However strongly we may sympathize with Adam's chivalry, however noble his self-sacrifice may seem to some, for Milton his fault was greater than Eve's, as Hanford and others have pointed out, because of his higher intellectual capacities. Although he deceives himself or tries to in the end, Adam at the moment of decision has not deceived himself. His resolution is to die, to sin and accept the consequences. His reason does not dictate false, like Eve's, but he ignores its counsel when it counsels true. Adam, who is a law unto himself but for the single prohibition, whose reason is his law, violates both laws—the prohibition and his reason. His fault like Satan's is the ultimate sin of willing to do what he knows wrong. Like Satan, although for love of Eve rather than for love of self or hate for God, he has chosen at least relative evil for his good. And like Satan's, his remissness is inexcusable to Milton, who says so in his own person and in positive terms at the beginning of Book X:

[10] See Chapter V, pp. 108–109.

For still they knew, and ought to have still remember'd
The high Injunction not to taste that Fruit,
Whoever tempted; which they not obeying,
Incurr'd, what could they less, the penaltie,
And manifold in sin, deserv'd to fall.

(X, 12–16)

Those who find Adam right in preferring Eve and turning his back on God will find Christian wrong in *Pilgrim's Progress* when he turns his back upon his family to seek his God. They may well ask whether they do not share in Adam's sin, preferring lesser goods to the greatest.

CHAPTER V

God's Justice

MILTON UNDERTAKES to demonstrate God's right to govern and the justice of his government. Satan says God rules by his thunder, describing God as a tyrant and usurper. If God is not the rightful ruler, his assumption of power and his promulgation of decrees are of course unjust. It is necessary therefore that Satan's lie be exposed and that God's right to rule be affirmed on grounds acceptable to men and angels. The chief grounds of his right are two: he rules because he is the creator and because of his superior merit.

First of all, because he is the creator of the Heavens and the Earth and all that is in them, God is of right the governor of them. They are his to do with what he wills. Out of his goodness his creatures were made. Since they owe their very existence to God, they have no claim upon him. His claims upon his creatures are infinite, simply because he is their creator. This is attested again and again. It is on a similar basis that Eve admits the sovereignty of Adam, her "author and disposer," whom "unargu'd" she obeys—because "so God ordains." It is exactly upon this basis that Sin agrees to open the gates of Hell for Satan's egress, disobeying God's command, and addressing Satan thus:

> Thou art my Father, thou my Author, thou
> My being gav'st me; whom should I obey
> But thee, whom follow?
>
> (II, 864–866)

It is as creator that Adam and Eve adore God in their evening and in their morning hymn, and it is on the ground that God raised them from the dust to place them in Eden in happiness that they, "who at his hand have nothing merited," accept the single prohibition. Satan in his great lament at the beginning of Book IV [1] admits that God

> deservd no such return
> From me, whom he created what I was
> In that bright eminence.
>
> (IV, 42–44)

Satan has earlier denied that he is God's creature and in so doing denies God's right to rule—in a significant context, when Abdiel has affirmed it. Abdiel's statement is most explicit of all. He is replying to Satan's envy at the exaltation of the Son:

> Shalt thou give Law to God, shalt thou dispute
> With him the points of libertie, who made
> Thee what thou art, and formd the Pow'rs of Heav'n
> Such as he pleasd, and circumscrib'd thir being?
>
> (V, 822–825)

This of God. Of the Son, too, Abdiel affirms the superiority on the ground that he was the maker, the efficient cause, through whom God accomplished the creation. The argument is so telling that Satan can only defend his rebellion not by denying the right of a creator to rule, but by denying the fact of creation, by means of the sophistic argument from lack of memory:

> who saw
> When this creation was? rememberst thou
> Thy making, while the Maker gave thee being?
> We know no time when we were not as now;
> Know none before us, self-begot, self-rais'd
> By our own quickening power.
>
> (V, 856–861)

[1] See Chapter III, pp. 35–36.

God rules by right of merit, also, on the ground of his infinite wisdom, goodness, and power. Both his merit and the right based upon it are also affirmed by Abdiel:

> Unjustly thou deprav'st it with the name
> Of *Servitude* to serve whom God ordains,
> Or Nature; God and Nature bid the same,
> When he who rules is worthiest, and excells
> Them whom he governs.
>
> (VI, 174–178)

This, of course, of the exaltation of the Son. But the principle is clear. God also affirms it as the basis of the Son's viceregency, sending Abdiel

> to subdue
> By force, who reason for thir Law refuse,
> Right reason for thir Law, and for thir King
> *Messiah,* who by right of merit Reigns.[2]
>
> (VI, 40–43)

The principle of rule by merit is an important one in *Paradise Lost* and in Milton's thought in general. To accept it is to accept with it the corollary that Satan's rebellion is inexcusable. One reason why it is so important to a proper understanding of Milton is that the identification of Milton and Satan with which we have already concerned ourselves has often been based upon their mutual attachment to revolutionary principles. The admirers of Satan have often perhaps been those to whom the word *rebel* is not a term of reproach, but one of commendation—who regard opposition to any authority as praiseworthy, and who forget that it is the father of lies who speaks of the "tyranny of Heaven." But Satan's rebellion is not a matter of principle. It springs from

---

[2] Cf. *Paradise Regained,* I, 166: "This perfect Man, by merit call'd my Son."

his own pride, from his personal ambition. The occasion for it is the Son's elevation.

There is some confusion here. In the first place, Abdiel explains the justice of the elevation of the Son in terms of his original superiority as the efficient cause at the creation, reproaching Satan for his assumption of equality:

> Thy self though great and glorious dost thou count,
> Or all Angelic Nature joind in one,
> Equal to him begotten Son, by whom
> As by his Word the mighty Father made
> All things, ev'n thee . . . ?
>
> (V, 833–837)

Yet God's decree that he has this day begot the Son, which provides the occasion for Satan's rebellion, comes much later than the original creation. The solution of the difficulty is doctrinal. It lies in God's figurative use of the word *beget*. Milton speaks of it in *The Christian Doctrine:*

for though the Father be said in Scripture to have begotten the Son in a double sense, the one literal, with reference to the production of the Son, the other metaphorical, with reference to his exaltation, many commentators have applied the passages which allude to the exaltation and mediatorial functions of Christ as proof of his generation from all eternity. . . . Certain, however, it is . . . that the Son existed in the beginning, under the name of the logos or word, and was the first of the whole creation, by whom afterwards all other things were made both in heaven and earth.[3]

The decree of the Father, then, against which Satan rebels, is not of the generation, but of the exaltation of the Son. It is his elevation to rule that is objectionable.

There is still a difficulty left, however. In Book III, chronologically later than the war in Heaven, when the Father announces his intention to create Man and foresees his fall, the

---

[3] Columbia *Milton,* XIV, 181.

Son offers himself as ransom. The Father addresses him as follows:

> All Power
> I give thee, reign for ever, and assume
> Thy Merits; under thee as Head Supream
> Thrones, Princedoms, Powers, Dominions I reduce:
> In Heaven, or Earth, or under Earth in Hell.
>
> (III, 317–322)

Is Raphael wrong, then, in telling Adam of the earlier "begetting" and in attributing Satan's revolt to it? That can hardly be. And there are two differences between this and the earlier: 1, the Son by his offered sacrifice, which none other in Heaven dared make, has actively demonstrated his (already known) superior merit,

> By Merit more then Birthright Son of God,
> Found worthiest to be so by being Good
> Farr more then Great or High;
>
> (III, 309–312)

and, 2, the exaltation now is not of the Son in his character as God alone, but as Man also:

> because in thee
> Love has abounded more then Glory abounds,
> Therefore thy Humiliation shall exalt
> With thee thy Manhood also to this Throne;
> Here shalt thou sit incarnate, here shalt Reign
> Both God and Man, Son both of God and Man,
> Anointed universal King.
>
> (III, 311–317)

There is then no necessary contradiction, although there certainly is apparent contradiction. Milton does not keep the distinction between the two occasions as clear as we may wish.

Unlike Satan's Milton's rebelliousness was based upon the

political principle that merit deserves to rule, a principle which condemns Satan's rebellion completely. Don M. Wolfe writes of it as follows:

To his analysis of the government of heaven and hell, of the home, and of man himself, Milton applied the leadership principle that he had so persistently championed during the tumultuous pamphleteering years.

The government of heaven, as described by Milton, accords ideally with the pattern of his commonwealth principles. Not, as Satan claims, 'upheld by old repute, consent, or custome,' but sustained by his perfection of character, God rules over all the aristocracy of Heaven.[4]

Wolfe then goes on to point out that it is so also in Hell, where Satan is "by merit raised/ To that bad eminence." There is point to the oxymoron, for in the topsy-turvy morality of Hell, the merit that can raise one to leadership must of course be excellence in evil. Upon this point Wolfe does not comment, writing instead that

Contrary to Satan's assertion, the angels of Hell have not exercised "free choice;" no more consent of the governed obtains in Hell than in Heaven. In his claims to natural superiority, however, Satan is fully justified: he possesses supreme courage, intellectual resourcefulness, rhetorical genius, subtle knowledge of passions and jealousies.[5]

But Satan does not have the prime requisite of the justly constituted ruler, virtue, the lack of which was in Milton's mind sufficient to justify the overthrow of the Stuarts. It is only in Hell that Satan's qualities fit him to rule. Nor does he rule in Hell without consent. Wolfe continues: "Gladly the inhabitants of Hell yield themselves to his will":

> He spake: and to confirm his words, out-flew
> Millions of flaming swords.
>
> (I, 663–664)

---

[4] *Milton in the Puritan Revolution* (New York, Thomas Nelson and Sons, 1941), p. 343. These passages are reprinted by permission of the author and the publishers.

[5] *Ibid.*, p. 344.

This, of course, of their ill will. Similarly, of their good will the unfallen in Heaven accept the government of God.

In the family too, Wolfe points out, man rules over woman by merit of greater strength, virtue, and intelligence. Finally, the principle is to be found in Milton's psychology, of which we must again quote from Wolfe:

Milton's conception of man's government of himself, like his conception of governments in earth, hell, heaven, and home, is colored by the domination of superior virtue and wisdom. Even here his philosophy of leadership obtains: the soul, being compounded of the senses, the passions, and the reason, should yield freely to the government of reason:

> Know that in the Soule
> Are many lesser Faculties that serve
> Reason as chief.[6]

The parallel is keenly observed, although we cannot agree with Wolfe if he means to suggest that Milton's psychology reflects his politics. On the contrary, Milton's ethic, including his political theory, is based upon his psychology, upon his analysis of the human soul and his judgment of the human individual. It is his faith in reason that leads him to affirm the supremacy of God (and of Cromwell), not his faith in God (and Cromwell) that leads him to belief in the supremacy of reason. In any event the political principle is clear, and its importance is clear. It underlies all of Milton's political activity; it is basic to the economy of Heaven, sufficient to condemn Satan's rebellion and to justify God's rule.

Here, of course, Milton's argument is circular. The goodness of God upon which it is based is the point in question. In assuming it, by definition, Milton is assuming one of his conclusions, not merely as an hypothesis to be tested, but as a premise upon which to build an argument. To be sure, the affirmation and reaffirmation are themselves important rhetorical means of per-

[6] *Ibid.*, p. 345.

suasion; and as the argument is presented in *Paradise Lost,* with incidents recorded not in chronological order, the reader hears God speak for himself (in Book III) before he hears the account of the great rebellion given Adam by Raphael in Book V.

There is logical proof of the point too, but this is also burdened by a question-begging device of which we must take notice. On the narrative principle affirmed by Milton himself that in a story the false speak false, we have carefully discounted the evidence of Satan. Neither his defense of himself nor his arraignment of God as a tyrant may be accepted. On the same principle, what God says must be taken to be true, and what his followers say of him. Yet it is God whom Milton seeks to justify. The one on trial, as it were, becomes the most trustworthy of witnesses.

Milton himself gives us ground for believing God: "Poets generally put something like their own opinions into the mouths of their best characters." [7] Nevertheless, the requirement of the narrative that God's goodness be assumed somewhat weakens the formal strength of the argument. We cannot dismiss this weakness by saying that no reader would be so perverse as to disagree with the assumption that God is good and the devil bad, for we have already quoted Shelley's disagreement; and Shelley is not alone. There is a check, however. In our examination of Satan's evil we do not stop with Milton's affirmation nor with Satan's words; for Milton did not stop there. We look at Satan's deeds. God too is an agent in the story. We must judge him, as we do Satan, by his deeds as well as by his words and by the praises granted him. We shall find that we have done so in the end. For the moment it is enough to affirm that it is because of goodness yet to be demonstrated that God rules. He and he alone is king by divine right. We may dismiss the Satanic charge of usurpation and consider the first step accomplished in the demonstration of God's justice—his goodness.

[7] *First Defence,* Columbia *Milton,* VII, 327.

The demonstration of God's justice depends also upon the demonstration of the freedom of his rational creatures. This is a troublesome point, for it involves the capacity of his creatures to disobey and hence seems in a sense to make the creator responsible for their disobedience. But the very capacity to disobey (as to obey, of course) is part of the perfection of a rational being. If God's creatures are so constituted that they cannot act contrary to his commands, there can be no virtue in their obedience. They must then serve necessity, not God, and are not rational beings; for "Reason is also choice." Indeed, the very function of reason is to guide the will in the choice of modes of conduct. Thus we have heard Adam tell Eve that

> God left free the Will, for what obeyes
> Reason, is free, and Reason he made right,
> But bid her well beware, and still erect,
> Least by some faire appeering good surpris'd
> She dictate false, and misinforme the Will
> To do what God expressly hath forbid.
>
> (IX, 351–356)

Reason and its operations end in action for Milton. Knowledge ends in action. We have already seen this in explicit terms quoted from *Areopagitica* and *Of Education*. We may repeat two sentences:

The end then of Learning is to repair the ruines of our first Parents by regaining to know God aright, and out of that knowledge to love him, to imitate him, to be like him, as we may the neerest by possessing our souls of true vertue. . . .[8]

And again:

I call therefore a compleat and generous Education that which fits a man to perform justly, skilfully, and magnanimously all the offices both private and publick of Peace and War.[9]

[8] *Of Education*, Columbia *Milton*, IV, 277.
[9] *Ibid.*, p. 280.

Adam himself we found described when first we saw him in
Eden as formed for contemplation and valor, for thought and
action. The two are not unrelated, and are part of the nature of
a justly formed rational agent. Freedom of choice on rational
grounds, then, freedom to choose good or ill, is part of the perfection of man or angel. Unless it be granted them, God's creatures are imperfectly created and God's justice is less than perfect.
It is a necessary premise for the explanation of God's later conduct, too. There can be no justice in the punishment, little mercy
in the forgiveness, of an involuntary sin.

Milton affirms the point generously. God affirms it at great
length in Book III, saying of man in predicting his fall,

> I made him just and right,
> Sufficient to have stood, though free to fall.
> Such I created all th'Ethereal Powers
> And Spirits, both them who stood and them who faild;
> Freely they stood who stood, and fell who fell.
> Not free, what proof could they have givn sincere
> Of true allegiance, constant Faith or Love,
> Where onely what they needs must do, appeard,
> Not what they would? what praise could they receive?
> What pleasure I from such obedience paid,
> When Will and Reason (Reason is also choice)
> Useless and vain, of freedom both despoild,
> Made passive both, had servd necessitie,
> Not mee. They therefore as to right belongd,
> So were created, nor can justly accuse
> Thir maker, or thir making, or thir Fate,
> As if predestination over-rul'd
> Thir will, dispos'd by absolute Decree
> Or high foreknowledge; they themselves decreed
> Thir own revolt, not I: if I foreknew,
> Foreknowledge had no influence on their fault,

Which had no less prov'd certain unforeknown.
So without least impulse or shadow of Fate,
Or aught by me immutablie foreseen,
They trespass, Authors to themselves in all
Both what they judge and what they choose; for so
I formd them free, and free they must remain,
Till they enthrall themselves.

(III, 98–125)

Raphael also explains the point to Adam, in Book V:

That thou art happie, owe to God;
That thou continu'st such, owe to thy self,
That is, to thy obedience; therein stand.
This was that caution giv'n thee; be advis'd.
God made thee perfet, not immutable;
And good he made thee, but to persevere
He left it in thy power, ordaind thy will
By nature free, not over-rul'd by Fate
Inextricable, or strict necessity;
Our voluntarie service he requires,
Not our necessitated, such with him
Findes no acceptance, nor can find, for how
Can hearts, not free, be tri'd whether they serve
Willing or no, who will but what they must
By Destinie, and can no other choose?

(V, 520–534)

And Raphael enforces the lesson with the telling examples of the
angels, true and fallen:

My self and all th'Angelic Host that stand
In sight of God enthron'd, our happie state
Hold, as you yours, while our obedience holds;
On other surety none; freely we serve

Because wee freely love, as in our will
To love or not; in this we stand or fall:
And som are fall'n, to disobedience fall'n,
And so from Heav'n to deepest Hell: O fall
From what high state of bliss into what woe!

(V, 536–544)

We have heard Satan admit his freedom, too (now lost in his enthrallment to himself) in the address to the sun at the beginning of Book IV,

Hadst thou the same free Will and Power to stand?
Thou hadst.

(IV, 66–67)

We have heard him, like Raphael, support the thesis by recalling that others fell not.

Milton cannot demonstrate by example the freedom of man to choose the right, for the story provides no man to stand while others fall, except in the vision of the future that Michael brings to Adam in the end. But a mere affirmation of so important a point, however often repeated, is not enough if example is also possible. Consequently we are given the telling instance of Abdiel to illustrate the freedom of the angels, who are like men in this. For it is exactly this, the freedom of the will, freedom of choice on rational grounds, that the incident of Abdiel illustrates.

When Adam falls it is because he places his loyalty to Eve above his loyalty to God. There is no romantic lover's code to excuse the followers of Satan in the eyes of the future, but there is a conflict of loyalties nevertheless. Satan is after all a great commander to whom his legions owe and give fidelity. When Satan's will is one with God's, obedience to Satan is right for his followers. When Satan is in rebellion, they must choose their course. This conflict of loyalties is as real for Abdiel as for any; yet

Abdiel alone of Satan's host chooses the right. Abdiel remaining steadfast, who can say the others could not?

Abdiel, rebuking Satan, bases his own choice of faithfulness to God not upon mere blind loyalty but upon reason. It is from him that we learn in part that reason, not mere force, requires such obedience, and, from Raphael's account of Abdiel, Adam might have learned it. It is Abdiel who affirms the principle of rule by merit, as we have seen. In enouncing it and in thereby besting Satan in debate, he provides us with an example not of obedience alone, but of the means by which obedience may be assured— that is, by reason. If we learn from his utterance in part that God and reason bid the same, we learn from his conduct and its sequel that reason is our proper law, as we learn also from his exposure of Satan's sophistries that Satan's disobedience, like Eve's and Adam's, is departure from reason. His final speech concluded, before his departure from Satan's host, it is for his adherence to truth, in spite of numbers and of false example, that Raphael commends him in his narrative to Adam:

> So spake the Seraph *Abdiel* faithful found,
> Among the faithless, faithful only hee;
> Among innumerable false, unmov'd,
> Unshak'n, unseduc'd, unterrifi'd
> His Loyaltie he kept, his Love, his Zeale;
> Nor number, nor example with him wrought
> To swerve from truth, or change his constant mind
> Though single.
>
> (V, 896–903)

When Abdiel returns to the seat of Heaven, God commends him in the same terms, for his espousal of Truth, condemning the others for their refusal of the law of reason:

> Servant of God, well done, well hast thou fought
> The better fight, who single hast maintaind

Against revolted multitudes the Cause
Of Truth, in word mightier then they in Armes;
And for the testimonie of Truth hast born
Universal reproach, far worse to beare
Then violence: for this was all thy care
To stand approv'd in sight of God, though Worlds
Judg'd thee perverse: the easier conquest now
Remains thee, aided by this host of friends,
Back on thy foes more glorious to return
Then scornd thou didst depart, and to subdue
By force, who reason for thir Law refuse,
Right reason for thir Law, and for thir King
Messiah, who by right of merit Reigns.

                                        (VI, 29–44)

Abdiel, we may conclude, stands exemplary to all mankind, a
model of conduct and a teacher of reason. If God's commendation of him has been thought sometimes Milton's commendation
of himself, it is a reflection of posterity's evaluation of Milton's
example, for in the poem the commendation comes with greatest
propriety both to the narrative and to the argument.

Given no example, man's freedom is nevertheless given as
positive affirmation as that of the angels. God we have heard on
the subject, and Raphael. And finally, Adam, who tells Raphael
he has known himself free from the first:

                                nor knew I not
            To be both will and deed created free.

                                        (V, 548–549)

For the sake of Milton's argument, the freedom of the will hardly
needs further demonstration. If the world, unfortunately, has
not agreed unanimously, it is only necessary for God's justice
within the narrative that God, the fallen angels, and man agree.
Neither Adam nor Satan is successful in his attempt to evade

responsibility, for neither can deny either his freedom or his sufficiency. Both try to escape, Satan lamenting at one point his former exalted position as a basis for his ambition, Adam suggesting to Raphael some flaw in his nature as responsible for his excessive love of Eve. But neither of them convinces even himself. Each decrees his own fall; each is responsible for the consequences of his fall.

Not all critics of Milton, however, have found the affirmation of man's freedom acceptable. Some have not accepted the affirmation of man's sufficiency. Some have been unable to make with Milton the distinction between foreknowledge and predestination. Some have accepted for Adam the excuse that Raphael refuses to accept:

> Or Nature faild in mee, and left some part
> Not proof enough such Object to sustain,
> Or from my side subducting, took perhaps
> More then enough.
>
> (VIII, 534–537)

"Accuse not Nature," Raphael replies, his brow contracted, "She hath done her part." To which these reply, she has indeed! Tillyard's estimate of Eve's "triviality of mind" is a suggestion that she has not been given intellect enough to resist Satan, and Sir Herbert Grierson is explicit in his refusal to accept Raphael's admonition:

not only the Mercy of which God speaks but simple Justice would seem to require some consideration of the human nature given to Adam and Eve, its limitations, before such sweeping judgements were endorsed.[10]

In this passage, Grierson is concerned, clearly, for the insufficiency of Adam and Eve. He strikes at the very heart of the

[10] *Milton and Wordsworth: Poets and Prophets* (Cambridge, England, Cambridge University Press; New York, The Macmillan Company, 1937), p. 112. Reprinted by permission of the publishers.

justification. If Nature did indeed fail in Adam and Eve, if their
limitations were such that they could not have stood, there is
nothing but necessity for them to serve, and we can find neither
justice nor mercy in the judgment. Nor are they then created
"just and right." Adam and Eve fell, and God foreknew. It is
very easy to say, with the wisdom of hindsight, that they could
not have done otherwise, being what they were. But it does not
follow. We may only conclude from the event, not that they
could not, but that they did not resist temptation. Our knowledge of the event after it has happened has no more bearing upon
its inevitability, its determination, than God's knowledge before
it. Milton takes every precaution to see that we follow this part
of the argument, affirming positively the conditional nature of
God's decrees and the difference between foreknowledge and
predestination.

Milton makes it clear that Raphael was sent to tell man of his
danger in order that he might be sufficient to withstand Satan.
Surely it is in part to make the reader aware of that sufficiency
that we are given so full an account of Raphael's visit. Hanford
observes that Raphael comes as if in answer to the invocation of
Adam and Eve. Still more clearly he comes in answer to the
foreshadowing appeal that Milton prefixes to Book IV in his
own person:

> O for that warning voice, which he who saw
> Th'*Apocalyps,* heard cry in Heaven aloud,
>   . . . that now,
> While time was, our first-Parents had bin warnd
> The coming of thir secret foe, and scap'd
> Haply so scap'd his mortal snare;
>
>   (IV, 1–8)

For the coming of Raphael provides that warning, by which they
should have escaped.

In the "argument" prefixed as summary to Book V, God's purpose in sending Raphael is clearly stated:

God to render Man inexcusable sends Raphael *to admonish him of his obedience, of his free estate, of his enemy near at hand; who he is, and why his enemy, and whatever else may avail* Adam *to know.*

In the poem itself as well, God states his purpose to Raphael:

> such discourse bring on
> As may advise him of his happie state,
> Happiness in his power left free to will,
> Left to his own free Will, his Will though free,
> Yet mutable, whence warne him to beware
> He swerve not too secure: tell him withall
> His danger, and from whom, what enemie
> Late falln himself from Heav'n, is plotting now
> The fall of others from like state of bliss;
> By violence, no, for that shall be withstood,
> But by deceit and lies; this let him know,
> Least wilfully transgressing he pretend
> Surprisal, unadmonisht, unforewarnd.
>
> (V, 233–245)

And Milton himself comments:

> So spake th'Eternal Father, and fulfilld
> All Justice.
>
> (V, 246–247)

How complete is the warning Raphael brings, in what detail it anticipates the impulses that lead man into trouble, in what specific terms it points out Adam's dangerous weakness, we have already seen. Thus forewarned, man is forearmed and should triumph. That he does not is a failure of reason and will for which he himself is responsible and for which no sympathetic "allowance" can be made.

The demonstration of God's justice depends upon the happiness of the faithful—upon the assertion, that is, that Man in Eden had at his disposal the requisites for perfect happiness. This too is generously affirmed, but not always believed. Tillyard for one observes that Milton

fails to convince us that Adam and Eve are happy, because he can find no adequate scope for their active natures. . . . Reduced to the ridiculous task of working in a garden which produces of its own accord more than they will ever need, Adam and Eve are in the hopeless position of Old Age Pensioners enjoying perpetual youth.[11]

As Tillyard implies here, Basil Willey affirms, that Milton himself did not really believe that

innocence would have been better than morality. . . . "Assuredly we bring not innocence into the world, we bring impurity much rather": this is what Milton knew and believed; yet his adherence to Genesis involved him in the necessity of representing man's true and primal happiness as the innocence of Eden.[12]

Perhaps, then, we should remain unconvinced by Eden. It is a delightful pastoral scene, and innocent Eve and Adam are charming pastoral figures. There is in the picture of Eden, certainly, some of the passionate longing for the golden age that led Paul Elmer More to find in it the central theme of the poem. But it remains a pleasant fiction for which we should hardly be persuaded to exchange reality. We feel that Milton himself, Tillyard says,

stranded in his own Paradise, would very soon have eaten the apple on his own responsibility and immediately justified the act in a polemical pamphlet.[13]

[11] *Milton* (London, Chatto and Windus; New York, Dial Press, 1930), p. 282. Reprinted by permission of the publishers.
[12] Basil Willey, *The Seventeenth Century Background,* (London, Chatto and Windus, 1934), pp. 247-248.
[13] *Milton,* p. 282. Reprinted by permission of the publishers.

But it does not follow because we are unconvinced by Milton's argument that he does not mean what he says. Even though he himself might have been unhappy in Eden, it does not follow that he does not mean what he says. It is not Milton who is stranded in Paradise. It is Adam and Eve. Milton in Eden, Tillyard is probably right, would be bored. And so should we. The question is not what Milton would do in the place of Adam and Eve, however, nor what we should do, but rather what they do. Not from boredom and not because they are unhappy, they eat of the forbidden fruit. And the "polemical pamphlet" that Milton writes upon the occasion is *Paradise Lost*, which can hardly be construed to be a justification of the act. In it, whether he fails to convince us or not, Milton intended to convince us that Adam and Eve in Paradise before the fall enjoyed all the happiness of which they were capable.

The ecstatic description of Eden, Satan's envy of Adam and Eve in their possession of it, and the importance given their regrets at having to leave it at the end of the poem are evidence of this, as are the explicit statements of Adam and Raphael; for example, Adam's wonder, already quoted, at the suggestion that he should ever want obedience to him

> Who formd us from the dust, and plac'd us here
> Full to the utmost measure of what bliss
> Human desires can seek or apprehend.
>
> (V, 516–518)

To which Raphael replies:

> That thou art happie, owe to God;
> That thou continu'st such, owe to thy self.

Milton, then, might not have been happy in Eden. We might not be happy in Eden. Adam and Eve were, to the full extent of human capacity, and could anticipate still greater capacity and greater happiness.[14]

The superiority of Adam over other creation, Raphael explains, lies in the gift of reason, in which the soul has her being. By the exercise of reason, man may retain and increase his happiness until he achieves the sight of God. The path of reason is the acceptance of God's will. Communion of will with God is bliss and the means to bliss. But it is from God's will (and from happiness) that Adam and Eve depart when, at the fall, appetite and passion are exalted above reason. This, the elevation of passion and appetite to control over reason, over the rational will, is their disobedience.

The fallen angels even more clearly than Adam and Eve give up union of will with God and exchange bliss for misery. When Satan exclaims that "fardest from him is best," he has taken evil for his good. He follows the exclamation with the farewell to Heaven and the salute to Hell:

> Farewel happy Fields
> Where Joy for ever dwells: Hail Horrours, hail
> Infernal world, and thou profoundest Hell
> Receive thy new Possessor:
>
> (I, 249–252)

Then follows the assertion that

> The mind is its own place, and in it self
> Can make a Heav'n of Hell, a Hell of Heav'n,
> (I, 254–255)

the implications of which we have seen.

The happiness of the faithful angels is perhaps as unconvincing

[14] See Chapter VI, pp. 128–132.

as that of Adam and Eve. We have a dangerous sympathy for
Mammon when in the debate in Hell he outlines the consequences
that would follow the publication of Grace:

> on promise made
> Of new Subjection; with what eyes could we
> Stand in his presence humble, and receive
> Strict Laws impos'd, to celebrate his Throne
> With warbl'd Hymns, and to his Godhead sing
> Forc't Halleluiah's; while he Lordly sits
> Our envied Sovran, and his Altar breathes
> Ambrosial Odours and Ambrosial Flowers,
> Our servile offerings. This must be our task
> In Heav'n, this our delight; how wearisom
> Eternity so spent in worship paid
> To whom we hate.
>
> (II, 238–249)

Miss Watson was unable to make Heaven alluring to Huck Finn,
and the prospect described here is not alluring to us. As in Eden
we feel the lack of activity, of something to do. But Mammon's
description is of himself. For him the situation would be intolerable as well as impossible. He, like Satan, has bid farewell
to the government of reason, and fails to understand that a grate-
ful mind by owing owes not. "Forc't Halleluiah's" are not acceptable to God, nor servile offerings, nor envious followers, nor
worship paid by those who hate him. Only because they are un-
forced are angelic halleluiahs and hymns of praise a sign of
heavenly bliss; because the angelic offerings are freely and joy-
fully given they are acceptable; because followers obey the will
of God from rational choice, from community of will, coercion
is unknown in Heaven; and because worship is by those who love
it is accepted. In all this there is joy.

Of that joy and of that communion

> no voice but well could joine
> Melodious part, such concord is in Heav'n.
> (III, 370–371)

The hymn of the angels at Christ's sacrifice and the promised elevation of man is an example:

> Thus they in Heav'n, above the starry Sphear,
> Thir happie hours in joy and hymning spent.
> (III, 416–417)

Another example is the hymn after the creation, as of course are all the hymns of praise in Heaven and in Eden. Adam's desire for knowledge is satisfied by Raphael (in moderation) on the ground that the increase in knowledge will enable him the better to serve God, "and inferr thee also happier." But the final statement that communion with God is happiness is uttered by the Son, his words reported by Raphael:

> this I my Glorie account,
> My exaltation, and my whole delight,
> That thou in me well pleas'd, declarst thy will
> Fulfill'd, which to fulfil is all my bliss.
> Scepter and Power, thy giving, I assume,
> And gladlier shall resign, when in the end
> Thou shalt be All in All, and I in thee
> For ever, and in mee all whom thou lov'st:
> But whom thou hat'st, I hate, and can put on
> Thy terrors, as I put thy mildness on,
> Image of thee in all things; and shall soon,
> Armd with thy might, rid heav'n of these rebell'd,
>
> .   .   .
>
> That from thy just obedience could revolt,
> Whom to obey is happiness entire.
> (VI, 726–741)

The intention then is clear. If life as it is described in Eden and in Heaven seems to us dull, it may be because we are neither innocent nor angels, or it may be that Milton has failed to translate into concrete representation the bliss he has conceived. If, as Tillyard says, Milton "does not convince us, as he means to do, that a state of innocence is better than an unregenerate state of sin," he still means to do so. The argument as it was intended remains complete. And if it comes to that, on such a point how many of us in an unregenerate world can need convincing? The question whether Milton believed innocence preferable to the condition of regenerate man we must reserve for the next chapter.

The God of *Paradise Lost* is not guilty of unjust usurpation of power. He has a twofold right to rule because he is creator and because he is best fitted to rule. He is just, for his creatures, men and angels, were created as they should have been—free to choose and to persevere in right action, with a sufficiency strengthened in the case of man by a careful warning of the danger facing him. More than that, men and angels are created happy; continued or increasing happiness is the reward of obedience, and disobedience results in misery. The agents involved are fully informed of these conditions, and each is equipped as a rational being with the powers necessary to enable him not only to choose but to distinguish between right and wrong.

In the abstract, then, Milton's God is just. There remain two questions to be answered before we can leave the subject, however: 1. What accounts for the difference in treatment afforded fallen man and the fallen angels, and does the difference in treatment constitute injustice? 2. If Adam and Eve are condemned in effect by their acceptance and subsequent violation of a contract, are the terms of that contract not only legal but also just? Are the consequences of disobedience commensurate with the crime?

God himself explains the difference between his treatment of

fallen man and his treatment of the fallen angels at the time he
makes the distinction and promises grace to man:

> The first sort by thir own suggestion fell,
> Self-tempted, self-deprav'd: Man falls deceiv'd
> By the other first: Man therefore shall find grace,
> The other none.
>
> (III, 129–133)

A real difference, surely. If Satan were alone in his rebellion, we
should need no further answer. But Satan is not alone, and for
his followers, the lesser devils, God does not make merciful con-
cessions; the Son does not offer to sacrifice himself for them.
Yet are they not like man deceived?

There is some ground on which simply to say "No." God's
words seem to tell us so, implying clearly that Satan's followers,
like Satan, are self-tempted, self-depraved—self-deceived, if we
will. Then Satan as leader and misleader of angels does not bear
the same burden of responsibility and blame that he does as
perverter of man. For God says, not Satan alone, but "the first
sort" are self-depraved. Raphael telling of the reception in
Heaven of the decree of the Son's exaltation says that "all seemd
well pleas'd, all seem'd but were not all," a judgment that may
well refer to others than Satan. Most significant of all, no such
complex and lengthy argument as that Satan employs in the
seduction of Eve is necessary to persuade his host of followers.
Abdiel alone resists. He is not seduced, nor is any special attempt
made to seduce him. Satan is then perhaps only the leader, the
worst of the bad but not yet the corrupter of the good. This is
apparently a real difference.

An examination of the account of the rebellion given Adam by
Raphael, however, shows that this difference between the situation of Adam and Eve and that of the lesser devils is not great—
and that there is another difference more significant to their guilt.

Satan broaches the subject of resistance to God's decree to Beelzebub. His speech ended, Raphael comments:

> So spake the false Arch-Angel, and infus'd
> Bad influence into th'unwarie brest
> Of his Associate.
>
> （V, 694–696)

Beelzebub, spreading the word,

> Tells the suggested cause, and casts between
> Ambiguous words and jealousies, to sound
> Or taint integritie.
>
> (V, 702–704)

For Satan's part, so high was his degree in Heaven that

> His count'nance, as the Morning Star that guides
> The starrie flock, allur'd them, and with lyes
> Drew after him the third part of Heav'ns Host.
>
> (V, 708–710)

To be sure it is not fatal yet, for Abdiel is yet among them and he is to be

> faithful found,
> Among the faithless, faithful only hee;
> Among innumerable false, unmov'd,
> Unshak'n, unseduc'd, unterrifi'd
> His Loyaltie he kept, his Love, his Zeale.
>
> (V, 896–900)

Perhaps Eve would not have yielded had an Abdiel been there to oppose his example to the serpent's. But can we from this assume the followers of Satan to be "self-deprav'd"? Surely not. Surely we cannot hold that Satan's followers are equally responsible with Satan for the war in Heaven when we remember the mythical

account of the birth of Sin and when Abdiel himself addresses
Satan as follows:

> Author of evil, unknown till thy revolt,
> Unnam'd in Heav'n, now plenteous, as thou seest
> These Acts of hateful strife, hateful to all,
> Though heaviest by just measure on thy self
> And thy adherents: how hast thou disturb'd
> Heav'ns blessed peace, and into Nature brought
> Misery, uncreated till the crime
> Of thy Rebellion? how hast thou instill'd
> Thy malice into thousands, once upright
> And faithful, now prov'd false.
>
> (VI, 263–271)

Perhaps we may explain God's relentlessness toward the fallen
angels and his mercy to man in terms of their different attitudes
after the fall. Certainly there is a difference. We have heard
Satan affirm and Mammon imply that a return to Heaven except
as conquerors would be intolerable. The acceptance by acclama-
tion of the plan of Satan and Beelzebub shows this attitude to be
shared by all the lesser devils. Adam and Eve, on the contrary,
are almost immediately repentant.

Milton, through Raphael, raises the question of the possible
repentance of the rebel angels, in discussing their attitude when
at God's command the uprooted hills return to their proper places:

> This saw his hapless Foes but stood obdur'd,
> And to rebellious fight rallied thir Powers
> Insensate, hope conceiving from despair.
> In Heav'nly Spirits could such perverseness dwell?
> But to convince the proud what Signs availe,
> Or Wonders move th'obdurate to relent?

They hard'nd more by what might most reclame,
Grieving to see his Glorie, at the sight
Took envie, and aspiring to his highth,
Stood reimbattell'd fierce, by force or fraud
Weening to prosper, and at length prevaile
Against God and *Messiah,* or to fall
In universal ruin last.

(VI, 785–797)

But the repentance of Adam and Eve is part of God's goodness
to them. That is to say, the advantage of Adam and Eve over
the devils in the comparison is due not to themselves but to the
operation of Divine Grace, which has "remov'd/ The stonie
from thir hearts."

The evocation of grace, of course, and the whole redemption
system, are outside the question of God's justice, strictly interpreted. They demonstrate, rather, God's providence and mercy.
The strict enforcement of the law as laid down in the beginning
is all that abstract justice requires. If God deals mercifully with
men, giving them more than justice, it does not follow that he
must give more than justice to the fallen angels. Like treatment
of those equally deserving or undeserving is no necessary element
of justice if none is given less than his desert. Give every man his
just desert, and who among us will escape a whipping? A very
similar point is given explicit statement in the *Christian Doctrine*
in the course of Milton's discussion of predestination. It does not,
of course, apply to fallen angels, since it is part of the economy
of redemption:

If then God reject none but the disobedient and unbelieving, he undoubtedly gives grace to all, if not in equal measure, at least sufficient
for attaining knowledge of the truth and final salvation. I have said,
not in equal measure, because not even to the reprobate, as they are
called, has he imparted uniformly the same degree of grace. . . . For
God, as any other proprietor might do with regard to his private pos-

sessions, claims to himself the right of determining concerning his own creatures according to his pleasure, nor can he be called to account for his decision, though, if he chose, he could give the best reasons for it. . . . That an equal portion of grace should not be extended to all, is attributable to the supreme will of God alone; that there are none to whom he does not vouchsafe grace sufficient for their salvation, is attributable to his justice.[15]

Perhaps, then, the inequality of God's treatment of his creatures in *Paradise Lost* is to be explained in terms of the inequality of the creatures themselves. Although Eve is the first sinner and the temptress of Adam, we found his guilt the greater because his intelligence and strength were greater. Angels are a higher order still and should be more proof against temptation. So much of the consideration for the limitations of human nature for which Grierson asks is given to Adam and Eve. But even Eve was strong enough and wise enough to meet all temptations had she so willed and therefore needs no special dispensation beyond the warning by the messenger angel. If any were to be given, it should come, like the visit of Raphael, not after the Fall, but before it. It is after the event, however, after the fall of angels and of men, that they are afforded the unequal treatment that we have still not explained.

The explanation grows out of the heart of Milton's ethic. It is in *Paradise Regained,* not in *Paradise Lost,* that Milton outlines most explicitly the hierarchy of values which underlies the thought of both poems. In that hierarchy, as it is outlined in the account of the temptation of Jesus in the later poem and as is frequently affirmed in *Paradise Lost,* the highest good, the good that transcends even knowledge, is the love of God, the proof of which is obedience to him, the union of will with his. There are lesser goods which lead to this in the world of men, notably knowledge and the love of men. Thus we hear Raphael tell Adam that

15 Columbia *Milton,* XIV, 147-149.

> love refines
> The thoughts, and heart enlarges, hath his seat
> In Reason, and is judicious, is the scale
> By which to heav'nly Love thou maist ascend.
>   (VIII, 589–592)

There are then two kinds of sin, two kinds of disobedience—that based upon the excessive love of wrong objects, and that based upon a failure to love the good. Eve falls through a desire, however mistaken, to improve her lot—to improve her social standing, as it were, by becoming a goddess among gods and by knowing what only God can know. Adam also falls through his preference of the lesser good, his preference of Eve to God. Although the logic of their deed implies it, there is no intention on the part of either to change the order of the universe, nor is there hate of God. Envy and hate of God, however, are the very springs not only of Satan's action, but also of the action of his followers, who like him can find Heaven tolerable only if they may return as conquerors. Like Eve's, we may say, their intention is to improve their social standing, but at the expense of God, the Son, and the faithful. Their fault is not like that of Adam and Eve the preference of a lesser to the greatest good, but a failure to love good, a hatred of good. From the beginning they seek to overthrow the established order and to establish the supremacy of evil.

The justification of the treatment of Adam and Eve is based finally on the contract with Adam, for God's pronouncement of the prohibition, and Adam's acceptance of it as reasonable and just, constituted a covenant. Grierson writes of it as follows:

It was altogether Milton's way to insist on finding an intelligible, a reasonable justification. But the defence is too purely legal. Adam, created free, and forewarned of what may threaten his welfare, chose, influenced by his love for Eve, to disobey an arbitrary command, a tabu, and thereby entailed on all his unhappy posterity guilt, and a depraved will which led too easily to fresh falls and the continuous degeneration of mankind.[16]

In its barest outlines, this is the justification, and we must agree that it is legalistic. Adam is a party to a contract, binding to his heirs, which he breaks. God therefore invokes the penalty clause, but in his mercy waives some of his rights, through the intervention of the Son. Grierson says the prohibition is arbitrary, is a tabu. Satan also calls it "suspicious, reasonless." But it is not that, and it is not merely a tabu. Lest the reader also think it reasonless, Milton lets us hear Adam accept the prohibition at the very moment when he first speaks of it in our hearing as "the only sign of our obedience left." God has spoken of it in the same terms in Book III, foreseeing the fall of man and predicting that he will "easily transgress the sole Command,/ Sole pledge of his obedience." He pronounced it to Adam in the following terms, as Adam reports to Raphael:

> But of the Tree whose operation brings
> Knowledg of good and ill, which I have set
> The Pledge of thy Obedience and thy Faith,
> Amid the Garden by the Tree of Life,
> Remember what I warne thee, shun to taste,
> And shun the bitter consequence: for know
> The day thou eat'st thereof, my sole command
> Transgrest, inevitably thou shalt dye;
> From that day mortal, and this happie State
> Shalt loose, expell'd from hence into a World
> Of woe and sorrow.
>
> (VIII, 323–333)

---

[16] *Milton and Wordsworth: Poets and Prophets* (Cambridge, England, Cambridge University Press; New York, The Macmillan Company, 1937), p. 96. Reprinted by permission of the publishers.

Milton himself, to make the testimony complete, at the end of the invocation to Book VII, asks the muse to recount what happened after Raphael had told the story of the fallen angels,

> least the like befall
> In Paradise to *Adam* or his Race,
> Charg'd not to touch the interdicted Tree,
> If they transgress, and slight that sole command,
> So easily obeyd amid the choice
> Of all tastes else to please thir appetite.
>
> (VII, 44–49)

For the rest they are free—and free here too, to choose, to stand or fall. For the rest, as Eve tells Satan in Book IX, "we live Law to ourselves, our Reason is our Law." Adam, when the prohibition is pronounced, accepts it, even though his acceptance is only tacit as it is presented to us.

Milton, like Grierson, recognizes the sole command as arbitrary. He found its very arbitrariness reasonable, explaining not the reasonableness, merely, but the necessity that it be arbitrary:

It was necessary that something should be forbidden or commanded as a test of fidelity, and that an act in its own nature indifferent, in order that man's obedience might be thereby manifested. For since it was the disposition of man to do what was right, as a being naturally good and holy, it was not necessary that he should be bound by the obligation of a covenant to perform that to which he was himself inclined; nor would he have given any proof of obedience by the performance of works to which he was led by a natural impulse, independently of the divine command.[17]

And again,

Seeing, however, that man was made in the image of God, and had the whole law of nature so implanted and innate in him, that he needed no precept to enforce its observance, it follows, that if he received any additional commands, . . . these commands formed no

[17] Columbia *Milton*, XV, 113–115.

part of the law of nature, which is sufficient of itself to teach whatever is agreeable to right reason, that is to say, whatever is intrinsically good.[18]

The justification, we agree, is legalistic, depending upon a contract with Adam, which he breaks. The agreement is that as a sign of his obedience he accept an arbitrary tabu. But neither the demand by the party of the first part nor its acceptance by the party of the second is irrational, as Grierson finds it:

For Milton *all* sin was revolt against reason, and unfortunately neither for Satan nor later for Adam and Eve is it clear how they revolted against reason, for no reason is given either for the sudden and apparently capricious exaltation of the Son, nor later for the capricious prohibition of eating of the fruit of the Knowledge of Good and Evil. Milton's conception of the action of reason in the field of conduct is too abstract. . . . What we gather is seemingly that the will of God, however arbitrary it may appear, is to be obeyed. *That* is reasonable. Heaven is a totalitarian state.[19]

Heaven is a totalitarian state—with a difference.

The theoretical bases for the duty of obedience to the head of a totalitarian state, to a dictator or despot, are a negative evaluation of the individual and the assumption that the dictator, if he is not actually infallible, is more likely to be right on any conceivable question than any or all of his followers. Since the dictator claims infallibility, he commits the sin of Satan, arrogating to himself both the attributes and the powers of God. His followers, accepting the claims implicit in the dictator's assumption of power, and preferring him to God, commit the sin of Satan's followers.

The obligation to obey God is based upon his infallibility and upon his concern for his creatures. The difference is that God *is*

---

[18] *Ibid.*, pp. 115–117.
[19] Grierson, *Milton and Wordsworth: Poets and Prophets*, pp. 116–117. Reprinted by permission of the publishers.

infallible. Those who apply their resentment of authority on earth to the economy of Heaven also share Satan's sin in denying God's right to rule. Because man is not God, because Heaven is not earth and because God is God, the government of Heaven is absolute. If God rules by right, as creator and as infinite in power, wisdom, and goodness; if the sum of happiness is to obey him and the depth of misery to disobey; and if man is further bound by an agreement to obey and is aware of the consequences of disobedience, then surely obedience is the rational way. We have followed Milton through a long argument to that end.

The arbitrariness of God's commands has no bearing on this point, as the motives assigned for the various disobediences make clear. Satan, we have seen (Milton following a distinguished tradition), falls from pride, envy, and ambition. And Satan himself, like Adam, we have heard admit the justice of God's ways and the rightness of obedience. Abdiel points out the unreason of his conduct. Satan, Raphael, Abdiel, Adam, and Milton all thought there was an obligation to obey God's commands, and they all thought disobedience a departure from reason and a source of misery. For Addison this was the whole meaning of the poem, "that Obedience to the Will of God makes Men happy, and that Disobedience makes them miserable." This is not quite all, perhaps, for obedience is not simple nor the will of God easily discernible. But this is basic. Milton thought the will of God could be determined (since God and reason bid the same) and that the consequence of disobedience was reasonable and just. Even those who do not agree entirely can agree that Adam in Eden in the pertinent point did know the will of God.

There is still something to say about the "mere tabu." If the act itself of eating the apple was necessarily indifferent, as Milton tells us, the disobedience was not:

If the circumstances of this crime are duly considered, it will be acknowledged to have been a most heinous offence, and a transgression of the whole law. For what sin can be named, which was not included in this one act? It comprehended at once distrust in the divine veracity, and a proportionate credulity in the assurances of Satan; unbelief; ingratitude; disobedience; gluttony; in the man excessive uxoriousness, in the woman a want of proper regard for her husband, in both an insensibility to the welfare of their offspring, and that offspring the whole human race; parricide, theft, invasion of the rights of others, sacrilege, deceit, presumption in aspiring to divine attributes, fraud in the means employed to attain the object, pride, and arrogance.[20]

In *Paradise Lost* we find no such tabulation, but we find implicit in the actions of Adam and Eve most of the offenses on the list. Certainly Eve's decision requires her distrust of the divine veracity, and certainly she believes Satan (to be sure, unrecognized) before God; unbelieving and ungrateful she is, clearly, not content with her lot; disobedient, obviously, both to God and to Adam; gluttonous, for she does not restrain her appetite at the last; lacking in proper regard for Adam, since she must either be lost to him or must entice him also into sin, and because in eating she is disobedient to him. Adam is moved primarily by excessive uxoriousness. Both are insensible to the welfare of their offspring; invading the rights of God and of their offspring, they commit a theft; they presume—Eve before and Adam after the fall—to divine attributes, in pride and arrogance.

Adam at one point protests (after the fall, significantly) the terms of the agreement, finding it too hard. He seeks to justify a release from it on the ground that he was not really party to it from the beginning—that he did not ask to be created. Annihilation seems to him a juster sentence than endless woe and woe multiplied in his offspring:

> Did I request thee, Maker, from my Clay
> To mould me Man, did I sollicite thee
> From darkness to promote me, or here place

[20] *The Christian Doctrine,* Columbia *Milton,* XV, 181–183.

In this delicious Garden? as my Will
Concurd not to my being, it were but right
And equal to reduce me to my dust,
Desirous to resigne, and render back
All I receav'd, unable to performe
Thy terms too hard, by which I was to hold
The good I sought not.

(X, 743–752)

But Adam cannot accept his own reasoning.

Yet to say truth, too late,
I thus contest; then should have been refusd
Those terms whatever, when they were propos'd.
Thou didst accept them; wilt thou enjoy the good,
Then cavil the conditions?

(X, 755–759)

This is to put the justification on a legal basis indeed, ignoring
as it does the justice or injustice of the conditions. Adam goes
on to discard his own objection that he did not seek creation and
admits the arbitrary right of the creator. He would not himself
accept from a disobedient son the retort, "Wherefore didst thou
beget me?" God's right is clearer still, the creation being not "of
Natural necessity" but of God's will:

God made thee of choice his own, and of his own
To serve him, thy reward was of his grace,
Thy punishment then justly is at his Will.

(X, 766–768)

This settled, Adam turns to the next difficulty.

Ah, why should all mankind
For one mans fault thus guiltless be condemn'd,
If guiltless?

(X, 822–824)

Mankind may well echo, why indeed? but Adam again rejects his own protest. "If guiltless," his question ended:

> But from me what can proceed,
> But all corrupt, both Mind and Will deprav'd,
> Not to do onely, but to will the same
> With me? how can they then acquitted stand
> In sight of God?
>
> (X, 824–828)

It is his last effort to escape responsibility.

> Him after all Disputes
> Forc't I absolve: all my evasions vain
> And reasonings, though through Mazes, lead me still
> But to my own conviction: first and last
> On mee, mee onely, as the sourse and spring
> Of all corruption, all the blame lights due;
> So might the wrauth.
>
> (X, 828–834)

Christian tradition accepts the punishment of Adam's posterity with him as just. In Adam, as he says, all men are sinners:

The sin which is common to all men is that which our first parents, and in them all their posterity committed, when, casting off their obedience to God, they tasted the fruit of the forbidden tree.[21]

Upon the phrase, *and in them all their posterity* Milton comments further:

for even such as were not then born are judged and condemned in them . . . so that without doubt they also sinned in them, and at the same time with them . . . undoubtedly therefore all sinned in Adam. For Adam being the common parent and head of all, it follows that, as in the covenant, that is, in receiving the commandment of God, so also in the defection from God, he either stood or fell for the whole

[21] *Christian Doctrine,* Columbia *Milton,* XV, 181.

human race. . . . For if all did not sin in Adam, why has the condition of all become worse since his fall? [22]

This is once more to argue in a circle. The justice of the punishment is proved in the last sentence quoted by deduction from God's justice. God being just, his judgment must be. His judgment just, God is just. The appeal to authority and tradition with which Milton enforces the point adds little:

It is, however, a principle uniformly acted upon in the divine proceedings, and recognized by all nations and under all religions from the earliest period, that the penalty incurred by the violation of things sacred (and such was the tree of knowledge of good and evil) attaches not only to the criminal himself, but to the whole of his posterity, who thus become accursed and obnoxious to punishment.[23]

This statement is supported by appeals to various expressions of the principle in Scripture and by multiplied instances from Scripture of sins of fathers visited upon their sons and sins of rulers upon their people, but they also add little. Milton does not go beyond mere affirmation and the appeal to authority except in the deduction of the justice of the principle from God's justice that we have noted; but Adam's acceptance of his own responsibility and of the justice of the conditions on which he accepted life in the midst of an attempt to escape the responsibility and deny the justice is most persuasive—persuasive in the same way in which Satan's failure in self-exculpation is persuasive. The intention is clear and the rhetoric is excellent. If the justification ended here, however, we should not be satisfied. According to the contract, all men are culpable in Adam, by a kind of bill of attainder. This bill of attainder we are reluctant to accept, since it is applied to us as Adam's heirs. We prefer to commit for ourselves the sins for which we are to be punished.

Milton speaks in the *Christian Doctrine* of the "general de-

[22] *Ibid.*, pp. 183–185.
[23] *Ibid.*

pravity of the human mind and its propensity to sin." [24] This propensity to sin is part of the punishment of Adam. It is part of the sentence of death. Of death there are four degrees, we learn also from the *Christian Doctrine,* the first of which "comprehends all those evils that lead to death," and the second of which is called "spiritual death."

This death consists, first, in the loss, or at least in the obscuration to a great extent of that right reason which enabled man to discern the chief good, and in which consisted as it were the life of the understanding. . . . It consists, secondly, in that deprivation of righteousness and liberty to do good, and in that slavish subjection to sin and the devil, which constitutes, as it were, the death of the will. . . . All have committed sin in Adam; therefore all are born servants of sin. [25]

The other degrees of death are death of the body, and death eternal, or the punishment of the damned.

By the terms of the contract with Adam, men are liable to all four degrees of death. It is the second with which we are concerned, because in discussing it Milton affirms the bondage to which the fall of Adam condemns all men. Like Adam after the fall, men later born than Adam are not completely free. Their reason is obscured; their wills are deprived of the liberty to do good. Adam also is certain that what springs from him must be corrupt,

> both Mind and Will deprav'd,
> Not to do onely, but to will the same
> With me.

> (X, 825-827)

Both the Christian tradition in this matter and Milton's acceptance of it are judgments of human nature. That man is born weak, with a propensity to sin, liable to the slavery of the senses and the passions, we can hardly question. That is simply the fact

[24] Columbia *Milton,* XV, 195.
[25] *Ibid.,* p. 207.

which the Scriptural story explains. If we object that we prefer to commit our own sins, the answer is simple. We will and do.

Nevertheless it is for imputed sin that we are deprived in some measure of the freedom to do good. This freedom we have already found essential to a moral being. Its gift to men by God is an important proof of God's justice. When God created men free, he created them just and right. If it follows that the progeny of Adam, slaves to sin and the devil, deprived of freedom and sufficiency through imputed sin, are not proper moral beings, they may well complain of the legalism of the justification and plead necessity for their sins.

But God is merciful to men as well as just in his judgment of them. Since his mercy and the instrument of it are part of the justification in *Paradise Lost,* we may conclude that, for Milton, God's justice is inseparable from his mercy. In the economy of redemption, man, damned for imputed sin, is saved, *if he wills,* by imputed virtue.

CHAPTER VI

God's Providence and Mercy

WE HAVE AGREED with Sir Herbert Grierson that the bare justification of God in terms of the contract with Adam is "legalistic." But Milton does not leave it there. At the very beginning of the poem, he stated a twofold purpose—to

> assert Eternal Providence,
> And justifie the wayes of God to men.

The sentence is capable of more than one interpretation, and I think it means more than one thing. Clearly the line,

> And justifie the wayes of God to men,

may mean either of two things: to justify to men God's ways, or to demonstrate the justice of God's ways toward mankind—that is, God's treatment of mankind. It probably means both.[1] The two lines as a unit (assuming the double meaning pointed out) may mean that Milton intends to justify God's ways by asserting eternal providence, the *and* being purposive. Then the passage construes, "assert eternal providence and thereby justify the ways of God." The passage may mean that Milton intends to do both things: 1. assert God's providence; 2. justify his ways. Again both meanings are probable. Hitherto we have separated the two

---

[1] Cf. *Samson Agonistes*, 293–294:

> Just are the ways of God
> And justifiable to Men.

points, taking the passage to mean that Milton is giving himself two tasks. Now we are to undertake the assertion of God's providence, and as we pursue the question we shall find that our objection to the mere legalism of the justification is very greatly weakened—that in the assertion of providence, the justice of God's ways becomes much more apparent.

The affirmation of God's providence is an affirmation that, foreseeing the end, God insures that good comes from the evil he allows. This Milton undertakes to demonstrate to mankind, as he has also undertaken to demonstrate God's justice.

That Satan, not God, is responsible for the existence of evil in the world, "author of evil," unknown till his revolt, we have argued at some length. But to end the explanation of the existence of evil there is to set up a rival deity who truly holds divided empire with the Almighty. Satan sometimes falls into this Manichean heresy, but Milton does not. To him such dualism is untenable. God is all in all. He does not instigate evil, of course; it does not result from any constitutive act of will upon his part. Let Satan have the credit. But even evil is by God's permissive will—in order that good may come.

All this is made explicit in the poem: At the beginning of the catalogue of demons in Book I, we are told that it was "through God's high sufferance" and "for the tryal of man" that the fallen angels were allowed to wander the earth. It is foreseen that by "falsities and lyes" they will corrupt the greater part to forsake their creator. When Satan crosses the abyss of chaos, Sin and Death follow him, laying the pavement of the broad highway to Hell, "such was the will of Heaven." Similarly in many other passages Milton embraces the difficulty. Two more we cite. Immediately after the chronicle of the fall in Book IX, Milton opens Book X with a statement of God's permissive will, and of his wisdom and justice in allowing evil:

Meanwhile the hainous and despightfull act
Of *Satan* done in Paradise, and how
Hee in the Serpent, had perverted *Eve,*
Her Husband shee, to taste the fatall fruit,
Was known in Heav'n; for what can scape the Eye
Of God All-seeing, or deceave his Heart
Omniscient, who in all things wise and just,
Hinder'd not *Satan* to attempt the minde
Of Man, with strength entire, and free Will arm'd,
Complete to have discover'd and repulst
Whatever wiles of Foe or seeming Friend.

(X, 1–11)

God himself affirms it, also in Book X, looking down from
Heaven upon Sin and Death wreaking havoc in Paradise:

See with what heat these Dogs of Hell advance
To waste and havoc yonder World, which I
So fair and good created, and had still
Kept in that State, had not the folly of Man
Let in these wastefull Furies, who impute
Folly to mee, so doth the Prince of Hell
And his Adherents, that with so much ease
I suffer them to enter and possess
A place so heav'nly, and conniving seem
To gratifie my scornful Enemies,
That laugh, as if transported with some fit
Of Passion, I to them had quitted all,
At random yielded up to their misrule;
And know not that I call'd and drew them thither
My Hell-hounds, to lick up the draff and filth
Which mans polluting Sin with taint hath shed
On what was pure, till cramm'd and gorg'd, nigh burst

> With suckt and glutted offal, at one sling
> Of thy victorious Arm, well-pleasing Son,
> Both *Sin* and *Death,* and yawning *Grave* at last
> Through *Chaos* hurld, obstruct the mouth of Hell
> For ever, and seal up his ravenous Jawes.
>   (X, 616–637)

Satan, who knew God and has not lost all his knowledge, foresees the event:

> If then his Providence
> Out of our evil seek to bring forth good,
> Our labour must be to pervert that end,
> And out of good still to find means of evil.
>   (I, 162–165)

We have made with Milton two affirmations: 1. Evil is by
God's permissive will. 2. God's providence is such that evil results in good.

The necessity for the first affirmation is twofold. If God cannot curb evil, he is not omnipotent, which is self-evidently untenable. If he curbs evil, he is unjust. For we have seen that the
freedom of his creatures is a necessity of their being created "just
and right." That is to say, they must be free to choose good or ill,
and a just God chooses not to interfere with the choice. To whatever extent such permission implies it, God is then responsible for
evil. But only to that extent.

The second affirmation bears upon the other paradox: if God is
good, infinitely good, how can he permit evil? Early in *Paradise
Lost* Milton's adoption of the mythical explanation of the introduction of Sin into Heaven is an admission (by precedent of
Plato) that the paradox of evil is insoluble, that here is a mystery.
The paradox is not removed—for Milton was not one to make
evil merely undiscerned good—but it is certainly lessened by the
affirmation with which we are here concerned: that God permits

evil in order that good may come of it—may be made to come of it, rather.

But for the demonstration, for the justification, affirmation is not enough. We must see what good does come. The lines following those quoted above from Book X read,

> Then Heav'n and Earth renewd shall be made pure
> To sanctitie that shall receive no staine.
>
> (X, 638–639)

We shall return to this, but we must first go back to the creation of man and his world in order to trace the stages and the means by which God's providence insures our good.

In spite of rumors in Heaven preceding the creation of man—rumors invented, surely, for reasons of narrative economy, in order that Satan may proceed at once to his goal—we have found it clear that the fall of the angels was the occasion for the creation of man. The first positive good to come of evil is the creation of man and his world. The world itself is good. Tried by long obedience, he and his world are destined both for better, for the union of Heaven and Earth into one kingdom. Thus, to the happiness of man, Heaven's loss is to be repaired.

But the trial of man's obedience does not have such happy issue. As a result of it, we left man nasty, brutish, and mean, fallen off from God, subject to passion and devoted to death, in life at least partially deprived of the freedom essential to his existence as a moral being. And we speak now not of Adam and Eve alone, but of the race, of the race condemned through the fault of its first representatives. Of evil, then, no good has come, but of good, evil.

Happily the end is not yet. Through God's mercy, because of his providence, Man's freedom is in part restored to him, and by God's grace he uses it to begin the long journey back to salvation. In the passage from the *Christian Doctrine* quoted at the end of the preceding chapter Milton does not, indeed, seem to think that the loss of the "innate righteousness wherein man in the beginning lived unto God," the loss which occurred at the very moment of the fall, was quite complete. Let us look at the passage again.

This [spiritual] death consists, first, in the loss, or at least in the obscuration to a great extent of that right reason which enabled man to discern the chief good, and in which consisted as it were the life of the understanding.[2]

The qualification, "at least the obscuration to a great extent," suggests that fallen man may by great effort achieve the truth and with it the true life. In *Paradise Lost* we find Adam making no such qualification in his judgment that what springs from him must be corrupt. But in Adam and Eve themselves after the fall, in their speech and in their conduct, we see that right reason is not completely lost to them. Immediately after the fall, of course, they turn to mutual recrimination and reach the lowest depth of their misery:

> Thus they in mutual accusation spent
> The fruitless hours, but neither self-condemning,
> And of thir vain contest appeer'd no end.
>
> (IX, 1187–1189)

In Book X, however, and later, we find consciousness of sin in both. Even in the passage in Book X that we have cited as Adam's attempt at self-exculpation, we also found him coming at last to self-condemnation. Eve too expresses her willingness to shoulder all the blame (and is again, quite properly, rebuked). Finally, in his rejection of Eve's suggestions of suicide and race suicide, Adam finds truth and the way to salvation:

> What better can we do, then to the place
> Repairing where he judg'd us, prostrate fall

2 Columbia *Milton*, XV, 207.

> Before him reverent, and there confess
> Humbly our faults, and pardon beg, with tears
> Watering the ground, and with our sighs the Air
> Frequenting, sent from hearts contrite, in sign
> Of sorrow unfeign'd, and humiliation meek.
> Undoubtedly he will relent and turn
> From his displeasure; in whose look serene,
> When angry most he seem'd and most severe,
> What else but favor, grace, and mercie shon?
>   So spake our Father penitent, nor *Eve*
> Felt less remorse.
>   (X, 1086–1098)

To be sure this is of God's grace, as we are told at the beginning of Book XI:

> Thus they in lowliest plight repentant stood
> Praying, for from the Mercie-seat above
> Prevenient Grace descending had remov'd
> The stonie from thir hearts, & made new flesh
> Regenerate grow instead.
>   (XI, 1–5)

So is it stated also in the *Christian Doctrine:*

It cannot be denied, however, that some remnants of the divine image still exist in us, not wholly extinguished by this spiritual death. . . . Nor, again, is the liberty of the will entirely destroyed. First, with regard to things indifferent, whether natural or civil. . . . Secondly, the will is clearly not altogether inefficient in respect of good works, or at any rate of good endeavors; at least after the grace of God has called us. . . .[3]

The passage that follows explains the relevance of this affirmation to the argument not only of the *Christian Doctrine* but of *Paradise Lost* as well. In it Milton deals with the clause in the contract

---

[3] Columbia *Milton,* XV, 209–211.

with Adam which deprives fallen man of freedom to do the right and which results in the punishment of imputed, in a sense, involuntary sin. Milton's comment is as follows:

There can be no doubt that *for the purpose of vindicating the justice of God,* especially in his calling of mankind, it is much better to allow to man (whether as a remnant of his primitive state, or as restored through the operation of the grace whereby he is called) some portion of free will in respect of good works, or at least of good endeavors, rather than in respect of things which are indifferent. For if God be conceived to rule with absolute disposal all the actions of men, natural as well as civil, he appears to do nothing which is not his right, neither will any one murmur against such a procedure. But if he inclines the will of man to moral good or evil, according to his own pleasure, and then rewards the good, and punishes the wicked, the course of equity seems to be disturbed; and *it is entirely on this supposition that the outcry against divine justice is founded.* It would appear, therefore, that God's general government of the universe, to which such frequent allusion is made, should be understood as relating to natural and civil concerns, to things indifferent and fortuitous, in a word, to anything rather than to matters of morality and religion.[4]

We have before now seen Milton base his argument for the justice of God upon the premise of God's justice. It is perfectly clear from this passage that Milton had not made up his mind whether the freedom he found in fallen man was a remnant or a restoration through divine grace. But it hardly matters. In either event—and the testimony of *Paradise Lost* favors the operation of grace as the proper explanation—the fact is evidence of God's mercy and in part removes the strongest theoretical objection to the justification as we have so far presented it. The mercy of God has become a part—and a necessary part—of his justice.

Still it is not complete. Man's prayers are acceptable to God through the intercession of the Son, but until the demands of justice are fulfilled by the sacrifice of the Son, man's regeneration cannot be accomplished. Through that sacrifice man is finally

---

[4] Columbia *Milton,* XV, 213–215. Italics mine.

restored to freedom, to his proper standing as a moral agent, and is to be shown the way to salvation. There is "poetic" as well as real justice in this economy, for just as mankind has been condemned for imputed sin, for the sin of the first man, so the race is saved by imputed virtue, the virtue of that greater Man who comes to restore us.

It is not in the "poetic" aptness of the arrangement, however, that we find God's mercy a support to the claim of his justice. We have found in the preceding chapter that the progeny of Adam are not moral agents in the true sense of the phrase in so far as they are not capable of choice, having lost to a great extent the "liberty to do good" in "slavish subjection to sin and the devil." This part of the covenant we have found less than just (however legal) on the same ground that we find it a necessary part of God's justice that men and angels be so created that they are free to choose evil as well as good. Unless they are created thus "just and right," their superiority over the rest of creation is nonexistent. So the constitution of later man, if he is denied the power of choice by the judgment of Adam, is not "just and right." He must serve necessity, not God. The partial restoration of his freedom partially removes the objection. God goes further. If man is to be saved by imputed virtue, it is by faith, through grace. He may will to believe or not, and the power of choice is thus fully restored. Free once more, free to determine his own end, he is left with no basis on which to cavil at the "injustice" of his maker.

This plan of redemption has been decreed from the beginning. It is explained in Book III:

> Man shall not quite be lost, but sav'd who will,
> Yet not of will in him, but grace in me
> Freely voutsaft; *once more I will renew*
> *His lapsed powers,* though forfeit and enthrall'd
> By sin to foul exorbitant desires.
>
> (III, 173–177; italics mine)

When the economy of redemption has been explained, God's providential mercy is explained. Michael promises that through the years before men are finally saved by faith, by just blood paid for unjust, they will be taught by law itself the imperfection of law, which is to be given

> With purpose to resign them in full time
> Up to a better Cov'nant, disciplin'd
> From shadowie Types to Truth, from Flesh to Spirit,
> From imposition of strict Laws, to free
> Acceptance of large Grace, from servil fear
> To filial, works of Law to works of Faith.
>
> (XII, 301–306)

Therefore not Moses, but Jesus,

> shall quell
> The adversarie Serpent, and bring back
> Through the worlds wilderness long wanderd man
> Safe to eternal Paradise of rest.
>
> (XII, 311–314)

It is the story itself of Jesus and his ultimate victory as recounted by Michael that completes the demonstration of God's providence, showing as it does how through his mercy the Son of God satisfies the judgment (preserving God's justice) and redeems the race. We cannot do less than quote this passage at length. It is after all the final statement in the justification, the fulfillment of Milton's promise to assert eternal providence and justify the ways of God to men, the end implied in the beginning of his argument. Thus good is brought from evil,

> Not by destroying *Satan,* but his works
> In thee and in thy Seed: nor can this be,
> But by fulfilling that which thou didst want,
> Obedience to the Law of God, impos'd

On penaltie of death, and suffering death,
The penaltie to thy transgression due,
And due to theirs which out of thine will grow:
So onely can high Justice rest appaid.
The Law of God exact he shall fulfill
Both by obedience and by love, though love
Alone fulfill the Law; thy punishment
He shall endure by coming in the Flesh
To a reproachful life and cursed death,
Proclaiming Life to all who shall believe
In his redemption, and that his obedience
Imputed becomes theirs by Faith, his merits
To save them, not thir own, though legal works.
                    (XII, 394–410)

The triumph of the Son as well as his sacrifice is recounted:

Then to the Heav'n of Heav'ns he shall ascend
With victory, triumphing through the aire
Over his foes and thine; there shall surprise
The Serpent, Prince of aire, and drag in Chaines
Through all his Realme, and there confounded leave;
Then enter into glory, and resume
His Seat at Gods right hand, exalted high
Above all names in Heav'n; and thence shall come,
When this world's disolution shall be ripe,
With glory and power to judge both quick and dead,
To judge th'unfaithful dead, but to reward
His faithful, and receave them into bliss,
Whether in Heav'n or Earth, for then the Earth
Shall all be Paradise, far happier place
Then this of *Eden,* and far happier daies.
                    (XII, 451–465)

Adam's response, which points the significance of the whole narrative and marks this as the conclusion of the main theme in the
formal argument, has given rise to a great deal of controversy
among Miltonists:

> O goodness infinite, goodness immense!
> That all this good of evil shall produce,
> And evil turn to good; more wonderful
> Then that which by creation first brought forth
> Light out of darkness! full of doubt I stand,
> Whether I should repent me now of sin
> By mee done and occasiond, or rejoyce
> Much more, that much more good thereof shall spring,
> To God more glory, more good will to Men
> From God, and over wrauth grace shall abound.
>
> (XII, 469–478)

The angel lets the doubt pass without comment. Has evil then
resulted in such good that the fall itself is not to be lamented?
Was it really a good thing? Should Adam really not be repentant?
The problem is one that has exercised and perplexed the minds of
the theologians as well as of the Miltonists, and we can hardly
hope to solve it here. We may perhaps not be able to determine
what Milton thought, for the question perplexed him too.

At first glance, certainly, it looks as if the fall were a good
thing. Mankind is to be received into bliss, introduced into a far
happier place than Paradise and is to live far happier days. Having learned his final lesson, he is to find a paradise within him
happier far than that from which he is expelled. Even his very
first sighs of repentance, the first signs of grace after the fall, are
described by the Son to God as

> Fruits of more pleasing savour from thy seed
> Sown with contrition in his heart, then those

Which his own hand manuring all the Trees
Of Paradise could have produc't, ere fall'n
From innocence.

(XI, 26–30)

All these passages look as though the fall were fortunate indeed, almost as though we might have assigned evil to God in the first place, as merely good disguised.

The question is perhaps not so important as it has been made —since, beginning with the premise that the fall itself was evil, whatever good may have come of it is but proof of the power and goodness of God. But the paradox is real nevertheless. If so much good has come from evil that there is more glory for God and more good will toward men, then the fall was good in the end. If not, if the lot of man and the glory of God are impaired, then has not Satan after all won a victory, brought if not relative evil out of good, at least destroyed some good, and thus succeeded in his aim of grieving God?

The consensus of recent opinion is that Milton regarded the fall as fortunate. That is the implication, perhaps, of Tillyard's certainty that Milton himself could not have been happy in the idleness of Paradise and would have eaten the apple. It is the studied conclusion of other scholars who have dealt with the question directly. We quote from three:

It is difficult, of course, to reconcile the idea of a world perfect before the entrance of sin with the statement that after the conquest of sin and death it will be succeeded by a "far happier place" in which man will enjoy a "far happier day" than he had known when fresh from the hand of God. But this is another of the contradictions proposed by the dogma itself, and it is authenticated in *Christian Doctrine* by an array of Scriptural passages. The recognized authorities were not quite agreed as to what would have been the portion of man and his world had he withstood temptation. Milton himself raised the query, but wisely refrains from attempting to solve it; he contents himself with the certainty that the bliss to be attained was greater than that which

Adam forfeited. This consummate providence is the climax toward which the entire revelation tends.[5]

The Adam who has sinned and through effort risen again is "happier far" than the sinless Adam of the garden. The nature of man was, it is true, originally good and pure, but the wisdom of human experience, and the excellence gained through suffering are still better. Nor is this an outburst of over-enthusiasm on the angel's part, for in the treatise *De Doctrina Christiana* we read: "The Restoration of Man is the act whereby man, being delivered from sin and death by God the Father through Jesus Christ, is raised to a far more excellent state of grace and glory than that from which he had fallen." This describes man not in heaven, but when dwelling on the earth after redemption and renovation.[6]

The latest opinion is Lovejoy's:

The Fall could never be sufficiently condemned and lamented; and likewise, when all its consequences were considered, it could never be sufficiently rejoiced over. . . . No devout believer could hold that it would have been better if the moving drama of man's salvation had never taken place; and consequently no such believer could consistently hold that the first act of the drama, the event from which all the rest of it sprang, was really to be regretted. Moreover, the final state of the redeemed, the consummation of human history, would far surpass in felicity and in moral excellence the pristine happiness and innocence of the first pair in Eden—that state in which, but for the Fall, man would presumably have remained.[7]

These are telling statements. But we are still not sure. Adam does not, after all, cease to repent his sin; he only stands "full of doubt" whether his joy in the good vouchsafed by God should not overwhelm—outweigh, as it were—his repentance. That he was right to disobey is of course unthought and unthinkable, for him and for us. Nor can we accept the presumption of the last sen-

[5] Cecil A. Moore, "The Conclusion of *Paradise Lost*," *PMLA*, XXVI (1921), 29. Reprinted by permission of the publishers.

[6] Allan Gilbert, "The Problem of Evil in *Paradise Lost*," *JEGP*, XXII (1923), 186–187. Reprinted by permission of the University of Illinois Press.

[7] Arthur O. Lovejoy, "Milton and the Paradox of the Fortunate Fall," *ELH*, IV (1937), 162. Reprinted by permission of the publishers.

tence we have quoted from Lovejoy: that but for the fall man
would have remained in the condition of Adam and Eve in Eden.
Milton gives us quite as much reason to think otherwise as he
gives us reason for approving the fall. In Book V, Raphael explains the hierarchy of creation to Adam:

> one Almightie is, from whom
> All things proceed, and up to him return,
> If not deprav'd from good, created all
> Such to perfection, one first matter all,
> Indu'd with various forms, various degrees
> Of substance, and in things that live, of life;
> But more refin'd, more spiritous, and pure,
> As neerer to him plac't or neerer tending
> Each in thir several active Sphears assignd,
> Till body up to spirit work, in bounds
> Proportiond to each kind.
>
> (V, 469–479)

So men and angels, rational beings, although the reason of one is
discursive, the other intuitive, differ not in kind, but only in
degree. Therefore men's

> bodies may at last turn all to Spirit,
> Improv'd by tract of time, and wingd ascend
> Ethereal, as wee, or may at choice
> Here or in Heav'nly Paradises dwell;
> If ye be found obedient.
>
> (V, 497–501)

In Book VII, when he announces his intention to create a race
to replace the fallen angels, God announces that his plan is to
place them in another world,

> there to dwell,
> Not here, till by degrees of merit rais'd
> They open to themselves at length the way

Up hither, under long obedience tri'd,
And Earth be chang'd to Heav'n, & Heav'n to Earth,
One Kingdom, Joy and Union without end.

(VII, 156–161)

God foresees, to be sure, that man will not survive the trial of his obedience. Nevertheless God's intention here is predicated upon the assumption that he will, and the future that is depicted is not different from the union of Heaven and Earth forecast by Michael which brings forth Adam's ecstatic gratitude. Surely then we may say that Milton thought man ultimately, and by degrees, would have been translated to Heavenly bliss and would achieve what man redeemed is ultimately to achieve: perfect glorification, which "consists in eternal life and perfect happiness, arising chiefly from the divine vision." [8] This is what he loses by the fall and this is what is restored to him by the sacrifice of Jesus.

But it is not with this happiness, with the vision of man living with God in a united kingdom of Heaven and Earth, that his happiness after redemption is compared in the passages cited as proof of the "fortunate fall." He is to know a happier place and a happier day, Cecil Moore says, "than he had known when fresh from the hand of God," to know a bliss "greater than that which Adam forfeited." But these are not the same thing. Heaven is a better place than earthly Paradise, which is its shadow. The ultimate happiness of mankind redeemed is greater than the happiness of Adam in Eden. But we do not know and Milton does not say that it is greater than the bliss he might have achieved, which is the bliss he forfeited. Indeed, we have seen the two consummations described in the same terms, and even in the passage from the *Christian Doctrine* that Allan Gilbert quotes, Milton does not compare the happiness that follows the "Restoration of Man"

[8] *Christian Doctrine*, Columbia *Milton*, XVI, 375.

with the happiness that would have been his, but instead with
that state "from which he had fallen"; that is, the state of innocence in Eden at the beginning of his history. In the same way,
the penitential sighs described by the Son as "Fruits of more pleas-
ing savour" are compared not with the fruits of man's obedience
but with literal fruits of the trees of Eden. And finally, the paradise within him "happier far" that Adam is to achieve even in this
life is not happier far than the happiness of innocence, but happier
than the merely physical paradise that he is loath to leave.

For all that, good has come from evil. Satan has won no partial
victory. We began the present discussion by saying that the paradox was real. We return to that. Lovejoy suggests that Milton
chose to keep two themes separate, the fall and the redemption,
so that in the first part of the poem he could show the fall as the
deplorable thing it must seem and in the latter could introduce the
idea that it was after all a *felix culpa,* using that idea to

heighten the happy final consummation by making the earlier and unhappy episodes in the story appear as instrumental to that consummation, and, indeed, as its necessary condition.[9]

This does not quite recognize how deeply rooted in Milton's story
(and hence in his thought) the paradox really is. Judging from
the care with which Milton, several times suggesting it, always
refrains from saying that it was a *felix culpa,* from the care with
which he presents the two prognostications of man's future—one
before and one after the fall—in the same terms, we must conclude that he was unwilling to choose between the horns of the
dilemma. With Adam he might say "full of doubt I stand" upon
this point, and like Adam come to no conclusion. Apparently he
had not made up his mind, and perhaps did not regard the question as important to his main argument. He had demonstrated
that the disobedience was itself bad and justly to be punished; he

---

[9] "Milton and the Paradox of the Fortunate Fall," *ELH,* IV (1937),
179. Reprinted by permission of the publishers.

had shown that the whole sequence of evil events stemming from Satan's pride and the various human weaknesses of Adam and Eve were turned through God's power and mercy to a good end. To assert eternal providence and justify the ways of God to men, he need prove nothing further.

CHAPTER VII

The Way of Virtue

PARADISE LOST outlines the proper mode of life for fallen man. Like Milton and like Adam after the fall, we live under the burden of sin. Therefore Milton writes for us. He intends us to make an induction from the example he has presented, to build upon his justification of God a way of life. The world that Milton's narrative interprets is our world, and the people in it are ourselves.

Faith and consequent obedience to the will of God are the basis of virtuous action, for Milton. It is lack of faith that makes possible the disobedience of Adam and Eve. When faith is lacking, the whole moral structure breaks down.

In *Paradise Regained,* Irene Samuel points out,[1] pleasure, wealth, power, glory, and knowledge are rejected by Jesus in that order, not because they are not goods, but because they are lesser goods—good, therefore, only to the good man. At the top of the scale of values, above reason and knowledge even, are faith and love, which alone can assure obedience to God. Raphael's injunction to Adam is crucial and cannot be overstressed:

> Be strong, live happy, and love, but first of all
> Him whom to love is to obey.
> (VIII, 633–634)

God must be first of all.

We have seen that Eve, in curiosity and vanity, breaks faith,

---

[1] "Platonism in the Poetry of John Milton," (unpublished dissertation, Cornell University, 254. To be published by the Cornell University Press under the title, *Plato and Milton*).

preferring knowledge and an improvement in her social position, and an apple, to God. Adam prefers Eve and an apple. In accepting this perverse scale of values, in preferring lesser to the greatest good, they represent mankind.

When faith is destroyed, "reason cannot know, the will choose, nor appetite enjoy in right and happy fashion." [2] As soon as Adam and Eve have broken faith with God, they become slaves of appetite and passion, losing the government of self. The first lustful intoxication ended,

> They sate them down to weep, nor onely Teares
> Raind at thir Eyes, but high Winds worse within
> Began to rise, high Passions, Anger, Hate,
> Mistrust, Suspicion, Discord, and shook sore
> Thir inward State of Mind, calm Region once
> And full of Peace, now tost and turbulent:
> For Understanding rul'd not, and the Will
> Heard not her lore, both in subjection now
> To sensual Appetite, who from beneathe
> Usurping over sovran Reason claimd
> Superior sway.
>
> (IX, 1121–1131)

When the Son approached them to render judgment,

> Love was not in thir looks, either to God
> Or to each other, but apparent guilt,
> And shame, and perturbation, and despaire,
> Anger and obstinacie, and hate, and guile.
>
> (X, 111–114)

This loss of love for each other follows from their loss of love for God. That being lost, all happiness is lost to them.

After the judgment, the first manifestations of grace appear,

---

[2] Irene Samuel, "Platonism in the Poetry of John Milton," 119.

and we watch the gradual return of love for God and for each other as the "stonie" is removed from their hearts. At the triumphant close of the poem their love is such that Eve can say to Adam of the banishment from Paradise that

> with thee to goe,
> Is to stay here; without thee here to stay,
> Is to go hence unwilling; thou to mee
> Art all things under Heav'n, all places thou,
> Who for my wilful crime art banisht hence.
>   (XII, 615–618)

Possessed of the paradise within (or at least with assurance of it) they then depart to fulfil the prophecy of Michael's last words, fifty lines before the end of the poem,

> That ye may live, which will be many dayes,
> Both in one Faith unanimous though sad,
> With cause for evils past, yet much more cheer'd
> With meditation on the happie end.
>   (XII, 602–605)

Michael's presentation of the future, first by vision and then by narrative, which results in this possession of all useful knowledge, all knowledge necessary to salvation, for all its most skillful use of example, makes more use of precept than any other portion of the poem except possibly the end of the passage which recounts the warning visit of Raphael. The two passages represent extremely skillful narrative management on Milton's part. Raphael and Michael are sent to instruct mankind. Naturally they speak preceptively. And thus with perfect narrative propriety Milton is enabled to introduce into his poem the precepts that clarify and enforce his example. In the survey of the future Michael shows Adam and us, by example, the results of envy and violence in Cain, the various forms in which death is to claim mankind—

in individual violence, by disease born of intemperance, in old age, in war. He is able to show us the dangerous joys and the consequences of lust and luxury, of tyranny, of idolatry. And he is able at the same time to give us the running commentary.

The whole account is prefaced by Michael's statement of its purpose, that Adam may

> learn
> True patience, and to temper joy with fear
> And pious sorrow.
>
> (XI, 361–362)

At the vision of the lazar house of death, to Adam's protest that man should be exempt from such deformities for the sake of his Maker's image,

> Thir Makers Image, answerd *Michael,* then
> Forsook them, when themselves they villifi'd
> To serve ungovern'd appetite, and took
> His Image whom they serv'd, a brutish vice.
>
> (XI, 512–516)

When Adam hears of the pains of death by old age, reward of temperance, he exclaims,

> Henceforth I flie not Death, nor would prolong
> Life much,
>
> (XI, 547–548)

and Michael responds,

> Nor love thy Life, nor hate; but what thou livst
> Live well.
>
> (XI, 553–554)

Adam comments upon the seduction of the descendants of Seth that man's woe begins from woman.

> From Mans effeminate slackness it begins,

Said th'Angel, who should better hold his place
By wisdome, and superiour gifts receavd.

(XI, 634–636)

When Adam after the flood rejoices at one man perfect found,
his judgment is confirmed:

Dextrously thou aim'st;
So willingly doth God remit his Ire.

(XI, 884–885)

When he sees tyranny, he is told (as we have seen) that true
liberty was lost with his original lapse in the surrender of reason
to government by passion. When he rejoices at the law of Moses,
he is admonished on the inefficacy of law and the need not for
works of law but for works of faith (XII, 300–306).

Finally, when the narrative has been completed, with the story
of Jesus, Adam expresses the first part of the lesson learned from
the examples and the precepts at which we have glanced:

that to obey is best,
And love with fear the onely God, to walk
As in his presence, ever to observe
His providence, and on him sole depend,
Mercifull over all his works, with good
Still overcoming evil, and by small
Accomplishing great things, by things deemd weak
Subverting worldly strong, and worldly wise
By simply meek; that suffering for Truths sake
Is fortitude to highest victorie,
And to the faithful Death the Gate of Life;
Taught this by his example whom I now
Acknowledge my Redeemer ever blest.

(XII, 561–573)

We too may learn from the account, if we will, the same
faith, by the example of Adam as well as by that of Jesus. And

we too may learn what Adam learns from Michael's response—
early in his last speech. It is his final precept:

> onely add
> Deeds to thy knowledge answerable, add Faith
> Add vertue, Patience, Temperance, add Love,
> By name to come call'd Charitie, the soul
> Of all the rest.
>
> (XII, 581–585)

These two speeches contain in formal terms the moral thesis of
Paradise Lost. This surely is what Addison means when he says
that obedience to God is the moral of *Paradise Lost*. The right
use of every good depends upon this filial obedience to God's will,
obedience based upon love and trust in his providence. This is
the one thing necessary to happiness. Indeed, the union of will
with God's is happiness.

Except for the single prohibition, the one sign of that obedience, Adam and Eve were free. Their reason was their law, and
God and reason bid the same. This is an equation that carries
with it many implications. The rebel angels in Heaven must be
conquered by force,

> who reason for thir Law refuse,
> Right reason for thir Law, and for thir King
> *Messiah.*
>
> (VI, 41–43)

It is here that the reasonableness of obedience, even, is most suc-
cinctly stated:

> for thir King
> *Messiah,* who by right of merit Reigns.
>
> (VI, 42–43)

Line ninety-eight of Book XII equates reason and virtue.

The knowledge that reason pursues (when it minds its own

business) is knowledge useful to happiness, knowledge that is or will lead to knowledge of God and will enable us to be like him. This knowledge Adam and Eve had before the fall, before their Maker's image left them; but this knowledge we must seek, with the doom upon us of knowing evil in order that we may know good. It is an arduous task. It involves first of all the moral obligation to be intelligent. It is not enough to employ our rational processes to arrive at wrong conclusions. Good intentions, even, are not enough. And there is danger even to the well-intended,

> Since Reason not impossibly may meet
> Some specious object by the Foe subornd,
> And fall into deception unaware,
> Not keeping strictest watch, as she was warnd.
> (IX, 360–363)

This is Adam's warning to Eve, and this is what happened to Eve when she allowed herself to fall into the train of specious reasons put into her mind by Satan, first in the dream and then at the tree. It was Eve's obligation to see whither her thoughts were leading, to see the consequences of her deeds, and to act accordingly. In this she failed.

But understanding is not enough either. Adam

> scrupl'd not to eat
> Against his better knowledge, not deceav'd.
> (IX, 997–998)

Intelligent enough, farseeing, anticipating the consequences of his action, knowing the higher good and that it was the higher, he departs from the government of reason, prefers the lesser good, and chooses to do wrong.

The requisites then are two: wary and active intelligence and an uncorrupted will. It is still not easy:

How happy were it for this frail, and as it may be truly call'd, mortall
life of man, since all earthly things which have the name of good and
convenient in our daily use, are withall so cumbersome and full of
trouble if knowledge yet which is the best and lightsomest possession
of the mind, were as the common saying is, no burden, and that what
it wanted of being a load to any part of the body, it did not with a
heavie advantage overlay upon the spirit. For not to speak of that
knowledge that rests in the contemplation of naturall causes and dimen-
sions, which must needs be a lower wisdom, as the object is low, certain
it is that he who hath obtain'd in more than the scantiest measure to
know anything distinctly of God, and of his true worship, and what is
infallibly good and happy in the state of mans life, what in it selfe evil
and miserable, though vulgarly not so esteem'd, he that hath obtain'd
to know this, the only high valuable wisdom indeed, remembring also
that God even to a strictnesse requires the improvment of these his
entrusted gifts, cannot but sustain a sorer burden of mind, and more
pressing than any supportable toil, or waight, which the body can
labour under; how and in what manner he shall dispose and employ
those summes of knowledge and illumination, which God hath sent him
into this world to trade with.[3]

Basic to the whole ethic is the doctrine of free choice and the
correlative doctrine of individual responsibility for individual
actions of which we have made so much. We make so much of it
because Milton does, primarily, but also because it is the fashion
of our age (and its greatest danger) to deny the inner freedom
in which Milton believed and the responsibility that goes with it.
For our age has accepted a determinist philosophy which explains
human weakness solely in terms of shaping environment and
heredity, and completely excuses it. We have already quoted from
Grierson a plea that "some consideration" be granted "the human nature given to Adam and Eve, its limitations, before such
sweeping judgments are endorsed." [4] Grierson is a generation
behind the fashion in appealing only to the "heredity" of Adam

---

[3] *The Reason of Church Government,* Columbia *Milton,* III, Pt. I, 229.
[4] Grierson, *Milton and Wordsworth* (Cambridge, England, Cambridge University Press; New York, The Macmillan Company, 1937),
p. 112.

and Eve, and not to the enervating environment of Eden, as Tillyard does; for modern sociology prefers to blame environment. But the philosophical determinism implicit in either explanation of human misconduct is wide spread. It pervades not abstract philosophy alone, but also much of our political and social thought, and the most successful of our contemporary literature. Certainly Milton would have none of it.

For in the terms of this philosophy or any other form of determinism, whether springing from belief in a predestinating god or from the acceptance of a mechanistic metaphysic, men are not responsible for their deeds. Praise and blame became meaningless, right and wrong nonexistent. The only questions proper about an action are "What is it" and "What (not who) brought it about." For in a sense one not responsible for his deeds does not do them. His grandfather does them, or the neighborhood in which he was born, or the fates, or the stars, or something he saw in the woodshed at the age of three. This is the weakling's effort to shift responsibility; and it is not only untrue, it is unworkable. Therefore even modern determinists, when they have the courage to deal with problems of conduct, affirm the necessity of acting *as if we had a choice,* and their ethic is based upon a fiction. Shakespeare's Edmund has a comment on the subject:

This is the excellent foppery of the world, that, when we are sick in fortune,—often the surfeit of our own behaviour,—we make guilty of our disasters the sun, the moon, and the stars; as if we were villains by necessity, fools by heavenly compulsion, knaves, thieves, and treachers by spherical predominance, drunkards, liars, and adulterers by an enforced obedience of planetary influence; and all that we are evil in, by a divine thrusting on; an admirable evasion of whoremaster man, to lay his goatish disposition to the charge of a star! My father compounded with my mother under *ursa major,* so that it follows I am rough and lecherous. 'Sfoot! I should have been that I am had the maidenliest star in the firmament twinkled on my bastardizing.[5]

[5] *King Lear,* I, ii.

Every age invents its own excuse, and the wise of every age reject it. Milton believed the human spirit capable of standing firm and uncorrupted in the presence of danger or desire and capable of rehabilitation if it failed. The requisite was that it accept the government of reason, and discipline itself. Unless we believe with Milton (and with Edmund) that we make ourselves, how may we hope for such self-discipline? We cannot discipline our grandfathers nor the horror in the wood-shed.

There is a political implication as well, contemporary with us in its reference. Ethics and politics were not separate disciplines for Milton, but parts of one. The angels who refused reason for their law had to be subdued by force. Throughout Milton's thought we find the political premise that, in order to be free, men as well as angels must deserve their freedom. When he recommended in 1641 that the magistrates should take over the management of "publick sports, and festival pastimes," it was in part to suppress "such as were autoriz'd a while since, the provoca-tions of drunkennésse and lust," but primarily in order that such entertainments be provided as "sweetned with eloquent and gracefull inticements to the love and practice of justice, tem-perance, and fortitude" might instruct and better the nation at all opportunities.[6] For the rest he was never done insisting that men must merit freedom to be free. What must we be to de-serve it?

Milton answers our question by warning the people of England that if they lose the freedom they have won the fault will be theirs:

For know that you may not feel resentment, or be able to blame any body but yourselves, know, that as to be free is precisely the same thing as to be pious, wise, just and temperate, careful of one's own, abstinent from what is another's, and thence in fine, magnanimous and

[6] *Reason of Church Government,* Columbia *Milton,* III, Pt. I, 239–240.

brave—so, to be the opposite of these, is the same thing as to be a slave.[7]

In the light of this utterance, it is well to examine some of the political freedoms most valued in our own generation. Freedom of speech and opinion is a cherished one, the one of which we hear most. Certainly it is the freedom of which the press and others of our more vocal elements are most jealous. Matthew Arnold valued freedom of opinion, too, the freedom of every man in England to say what he likes. But Arnold would not rest satisfied, he said, "unless what men say, when they may say what they like, is worth saying,—has good in it, and more good than bad." Surely freedom of speech is easier to maintain, and more valuable, among a wise people. What is said will be worth saying. Opinions freely held will not be nonsense. We need no demonstration, after *Areopagitica,* that Milton treasured freedom of expression, too, but he agreed with us and Arnold. "Do you, therefore," he said to the people of England, "Do you, therefore, who have the wish to remain free, either begin with being wise, or repent without delay." [8]

We hear much, also, of our cherished freedom to worship as we choose. His Grace the Metropolitan Benjamin began a speech on freedom of religion in Russia broadcast in the autumn of 1942 in New York City by saying,

I confess I am a little tired of speaking about freedom of religion in Russia. Why is it, I sometimes ask myself, that so many people—and especially journalists—ask about freedom of religion in the Soviet Union? Are they themselves so religious that they are deeply concerned about freedom of religion even in a foreign country?

It is a searching question, to which we must wish we could return a proper answer. Surely we are right to value our freedom of faith. But surely, too, it would be more valuable if we were

---

[7] *Second Defence,* Columbia *Milton,* VIII, 249–251.
[8] *Ibid.,* p. 251.

a religious people, and must be of greatest value among people of the greatest faith.

Let us pursue our contemporary reference a little further and examine briefly the other "freedoms" which have lately been often on our tongues. "Freedom from want" is not a political freedom, although it may be antecedent to political freedom. The hungry, like the gluttonous, are slaves to their bellies and thus lose the dignity inherent in human personality and with it the freedom to govern themselves by reason. Although they are poles apart in our sympathy, both the hungry man and the glutton are in a sense slaves to appetite and are less than men. Absence of want we must seek for all the world. It will be easier to achieve, easier to maintain, and better worth having when men have learned temperance. Waste, luxury, excess, offspring of selfishness and greed, are themselves evil. They are also enemies to plenty.

We seek to build a world in which there will be nothing to fear. Yet a nation which has nothing to fear, on good authority, save fear itself, may yet be fearful. To be free from fear, we must first be brave. Those who are free from fear because their courage is beyond fear have heroic virtue. We cannot all be heroes or martyrs, but it is apparent that "freedom from fear" cannot be the possession of a craven people. It would not be worth the price if it cost us our courage.

Each of these four "freedoms," then, must be based upon a positive virtue. Freedom from want implies temperance as well as industry; freedom from fear, courage; freedom of opinion, wisdom; freedom of worship, faith. All of them are based upon the selflessness, the magnanimity, that recognizes the dignity of the human individual.

We have of late forgotten the belief that "that government is best that governs least," but it was a noble paradox based upon the doctrine that the function of government is so to develop the self-discipline of its people as to render the discipline of law unnecessary. Laws against murder restrict the freedom of the murderer alone. Laws against perjury place no restraint upon the truthful. Laws against drunkenness do no violence to the temperate. Because prohibition imposed upon the freedom of the temperate, it failed, and made lawlessness fashionable. Yet the law itself grew out of our own intemperance:

it comes to pass, that the nation, which has been incapable of governing and ordering itself, and has delivered itself up to the slavery of its own lusts, is itself delivered over, against its will, to other masters.[9]

Too often today we use the word self-government to mean not government of self, but the possession of a voice in the government of others. Yet discipline of one's self is the first requirement of freedom for one's self and is essential to the freedom of others. The lawless, the undisciplined, the greedy, the bigoted, the cowardly, the brutal, and the foolish work ill to themselves and to their fellows, given freedom.

Libertie hath a sharp and double edge fitt onelie to be handl'd by just and vertuous men, to bad and dissolute it becomes a mischief unwieldie in thir own hands.[10]

When Leonard Philaras asked Milton to write a plea for assistance to the Greeks against their Ottoman oppressors, Milton refused, writing in reply that

There is, however, something else besides to be tried, and in my judgment far the most important: namely that someone should, if possible, arouse and rekindle in the minds of the Greeks, by the relation of that old story, the old Greek valour itself, the old industry, the old patience of labour.[11]

When in their struggles of the nineteenth century the Greeks showed that they had aroused and rekindled in themselves the

[9] *Second Defence,* Columbia *Milton,* VIII, 251.
[10] "The Digression," in *The History of Britain,* Columbia *Milton,* X, 324.
[11] Letter to Philaras, Columbia *Milton,* XII, 59.

old valor, they commanded the admiration of the world. A college town in our own country is named for the leader of one of the first uprisings, Prince Ypsilanti. Lord Byron was but one among thousands of volunteers from outside Greece who came to her assistance. In the end, Britain, France, and Russia gave their aid, and the war of Greek independence was won. That they and we have reason in the twentieth century to rejoice in the rekindling of the old Greek valor we need hardly say. Yet surely Milton was right that without the old Greek virtues, freedom would be useless and impossible to the Greeks.

This was the lesson that Milton himself, believing it all the while, had to learn anew from the Restoration. The revolution in which Milton took part, for which he gave up years of his poetic career and to which he sacrificed his eyesight, whatever we may think of the particular dictatorship to which it led, began as a democratic movement. It grew out of the seventeenth-century forces and ideas to which modern democracy must be traced in part, and it resulted in the limitation of royal power which has made English democracy possible. Even when it became most autocratic, the concern of many of its adherents (Milton among them) was to force freedom upon the world. But of course they failed. And their failure resulted in disillusionment for Milton. Certainly the terms in which he writes, upon the eve of the Restoration, of a "Shroving-time first, wherin to speak freely and take our leaves of Libertie" before "so long a Lent of Servitude" [12] are disillusioned terms. After the Restoration his despair seems complete in his letter to Peter Heimbach in 1666, in reply to a compliment upon (among other things) his statecraft:

For what you call *policy,* but I would rather have you call *loyalty to one's country*—this particular lass, after inveigling me with her fair name, has almost expatriated me, so to speak. The chorus of the rest [of

[12] *The Ready and Easy Way to Establish a Free Commonwealth,* Columbia *Milton,* VI, 111–112.

the virtues], however, makes a very fine harmony. One's country is wherever it is well with one.[13]

But this apparent disillusionment does not move Milton to give up the cause of liberty. On the contrary, it leads him to a still stronger conviction that liberty must be deserved, that it must come not from without, but from within, and that men achieve the political system they deserve. A bad government, therefore, is a judgment upon the governed. Political servitude but reflects the servitude of the soul to passion. Thus Michael to Adam:

> Since thy original lapse, true Libertie
> Is lost, which alwayes with right Reason dwells
> Twinn'd, and from her hath no dividual being:
> Reason in man obscur'd, or not obeyd,
> Immediately inordinate desires
> And upstart Passions catch the Government
> From Reason, and to servitude reduce
> Man till then free. Therefore since hee permits
> Within himself unworthie Powers to reign
> Over free Reason, God in Judgement just
> Subjects him from without to violent Lords;
> Who oft as undeservedly enthrall
> His outward freedom: Tyrannie must be,
> Though to the Tyrant thereby no excuse.
> Yet somtimes Nations will decline so low
> From vertue, which is reason, that no wrong,
> But Justice, and some fatal curse annext
> Deprives them of thir outward libertie,
> Thir inward lost.

(XII, 83–101)

The application of this passage is not directly to England, of course, but most readers will think Milton has England in his

[13] Columbia *Milton,* XII, 115.

eye. In any event, it follows that England has lost political liberty because her people have lost the freedom of virtue. The *History of Britain* confirms the application:

> . . . They who but of late were extoll'd as great deliverers, and had a people wholly at thir devotion, by so discharging thir trust as wee see, did not onely weak'n and unfitt themselves to be dispencers of what libertie they pretended, but unfitted also the people, now growne worse & more disordinate, to receave or to digest any libertie at all. For stories teach us that libertie sought out of season in a corrupt and degenerate age brought Rome it self into further slaverie. For libertie hath a sharp and double edge fitt onelie to be handl'd by just and vertuous men, to bad and dissolute it becomes a mischief unwieldie in their own hands.[14]

"In *Paradise Lost* and *Regained*," the anonymous biographer says, Milton "more especially taught all virtue." We have said it, too, and have found Milton saying that it is the function of poetry. For Milton to turn to that task is not for him to give up the political activity that occupied him from 1641 to 1655. On the contrary, it represents a recognition on his part that he has for those years had hold of the wrong end of the stick. It involves the resolution to begin over, after long years of effort resulting in failure and disillusionment, taking first things first. The system of ethics must precede the politics; ethical doctrine and the moral life are basic to all freedom. Before all else men must be freed from bondage to themselves. The first step toward political freedom is to make men just.

Milton reminds us also that this basic struggle for freedom is an endless one in which we retreat when we do not advance. The belief that it is so and that it is yet worth the cost is not the least part of our democratic heritage. But it is a belief with which our lives are not always in accord. Having fought with arms, we must not forget that even victory does not end the struggle. If the struggle ends with the end of the war, we shall

[14] Columbia *Milton*, X, 323–324.

have been defeated. But the enemy we must fight against now is from within. If now, when the war is won, we relax into self-sufficiency and pride, give way to passion and greed, indifference and sloth, accepting the government of stupidity and ignorance instead of reason, we shall have lost our victory. The warning voice of Milton told the people of England that

. . . as for you, citizens, it is of no small concern, what manner of men ye are, whether to acquire, or to keep possession of your liberty. Unless your liberty be of that kind, which can neither be gotten, nor taken away by arms; and that alone is such, which, springing from piety, justice, temperance, in fine, from real virtue, shall take deep and intimate root in your minds; you may be assured, there will not be wanting one, who, even without arms, will speedily deprive you of what is your boast to have gained by force of arms. Many were made greater by the war, whom the peace has again made less. If, after putting an end to the war, you neglect the arts of peace; if war be your peace and liberty, war alone your virtue, your highest glory, you will find, believe me, that your greatest enemy is peace itself; peace itself will be by far your hardest warfare, and what you think liberty will prove to be your slavery. . . . Unless you banish avarice, ambition, luxury from your thoughts, and all excess even from your families, the tyrant, whom you imagined was to be sought abroad, and in the field, you will find at home, you will find within, and that a more inexorable one; yea, tyrants without number will be daily engendered in your own breasts, that are not to be borne. Conquer these first; this is the warfare of peace; these are victories, hard, it is true, but bloodless; more glorious far than the warlike and the bloody. If ye are not victors here also, that enemy and tyrant, whom you so late have conquered in the field, you have either not conquered at all, or have conquered to no purpose.[15]

It comes to this. By persevering effort, by intelligence and self-discipline, prudence and temperance, fortitude and justice, by faith, hope and charity, we may achieve the individual and communal happiness that is the reward of virtue in men and in nations.

[15] *Second Defence,* Columbia *Milton,* VIII, 239–243.

Milton has undertaken in his poem to

assert Eternal Providence
And justifie the wayes of God to men.

His narrative and its argument are there for all to read. He knew—and for his knowledge has been called arrogant—that not all men would read, and consequently implored his muse to find fit audience though few. Ours would be a better world if that fit audience were not so few.

Index